dale
earnhardt

Defining Moments
of a NASCAR Legend

TRIUMPH
B O O K S

Copyright © 2011 by Street & Smith's Sports Group

No part of this publication may be reproduced, stored in a retrieval system, or transmitted in any form by any means, electronic, mechanical, photocopying, or otherwise, without the prior written permission of the publisher, Triumph Books, 542 South Dearborn Street, Suite 750, Chicago, Illinois 60605.

Triumph Books and colophon are registered trademarks of Random House, Inc.

This book is available in quantity at special discounts for your group or organization. For further information, contact:

Triumph Books
542 South Dearborn Street
Suite 750
Chicago, Illinois 60605
(312) 939-3330
Fax (312) 663-3557
www.triumphbooks.com

Printed in U.S.A.
ISBN: 978-1-60078-573-3
Design by Patricia Frey

All photos: David Chobat, Jim Fluharty and NASCAR Illustrated Archive.

Contents

# Introduction

NASCAR has undergone seismic changes in the ten years since we listened to NASCAR president Mike Helton deliver the news of Dale Earnhardt's tragic death on the high banks of Daytona on February 18, 2001.

The NASCAR of 2011 would be nearly unrecognizable to the legendary Earnhardt. The series, sponsors, cars—even how a champion is determined—have all been altered. Tracks have lost dates or had them shifted to make way for expansion to Chicago, Kansas, and Las Vegas.

In 2003, Brian France replaced his father, Bill France Jr., as NASCAR's chairman and CEO. And Winston, long the sport's most ubiquitous supporter, was replaced by NEXTEL (now Sprint) as the Cup Series sponsor in a 10-year $750 million deal.

The 10-race Chase format to determine the championship in NASCAR's top series was launched in 2004, with Kurt Busch winning the inaugural NEXTEL Cup.

In 2005, NASCAR imposed a four-car team limit in an effort to slow the dominance of multi-car team organizations.

To improve safety, encourage tighter racing, and lower operating costs in a flagging economy, NASCAR unveiled its "Car of Tomorrow" in 2006, and a year later instituted a "no testing" policy.

Toyota began competing in NASCAR's two top series in 2007, and in 2008 delivered the first Cup Series victory for a foreign manufacturer since 1954 when Al Keller won in a Jaguar at Linden Airport in New Jersey.

Also in 2007, Bill France Jr., whose vision and passion guided NASCAR for more than 35 years, passed away at the age of 74.

In a move that shocked the sport, Dale Earnhardt Jr. left Dale Earnhardt Incorporated, the team his father started, for Hendrick Motorsports in 2008 after a failed attempt to gain control of the operation from his stepmother, Teresa Earnhardt.

Jimmie Johnson, just a Cup rookie in 2001, is now a five-time champion mentioned among the greatest drivers of all time.

The digital revolution has inexorably altered the way we communicate. Can anyone imagine The Intimidator "Tweeting?"

One thing that hasn't changed is Earnhardt's iconic presence. The Man in Black is still the man. As a celebration of his life and legacy, we have collected the 25 most defining wins of Dale Earnhardt's career and present each in its original form, as reported by *NASCAR Scene*. ∎

— Michael J. Fresina

Earnhardt hoists his first Grand National trophy after taking the checkered flag at the Southeastern 500.

Earnhardt Wins Southeastern 500

First Rookie Winner Since Ross' 1974 Martinsville Victory

The first of 76. And it wasn't like he was driving for the Hendrick Motorsports of the day. He was driving for team owner Rod Osterlund, who brought a career record of 0-for-80 into the Bristol race. It should surprise no one that Earnhardt was the first rookie in five seasons to win at the Cup level.

They have been saying that rookie driver Dale Earnhardt (Kannapolis, N.C.) will someday reach the pinnacle of NASCAR Grand National racing.

He got there sooner than expected.

Driving the Jake Elder-prepared, Rod Osterlund Monte Carlo, Earnhardt more than fulfilled his promise Sunday by winning the Southeastern 500 at Bristol International Raceway.

In doing so, Earnhardt became the first rookie to win a Grand National race since Earl Ross' victory in the 1974 Old Dominion 500 at Martinsville – some 132 races ago.

"I'll probably believe it in the morning," said the excited Earnhardt. "This is a bigger thrill than my first-ever racing victory. This was a win in the big leagues, against the top-caliber drivers. It wasn't some dirt track back at home."

A combination of hard driving, excellent pit work and a smooth-handling car gave Earnhardt a triumph in only his sixteenth Grand National start. Earnhardt was quick to praise the skill of crew chief Elder and the Osterlund pit crew for his 2.7-second win over Bobby Allison's Bud Moore Thunderbird.

"The pit crew got me the win," said the 27-year-old Earnhardt. "When I was racing Darrell [Waltrip] at the end, they got me out ahead of him. I could build up a lead through the traffic, and I could tell I was getting farther ahead. After a while, I stopped looking in the mirror for him. I didn't look at nothing until the checkered flag.

"I kept thinking, 'This has got to be it.'"

Elder, who joined the Osterlund team just three races ago in Atlanta, said, "The boy [Earnhardt] ran a hard race. We had a few handling problems at the start, but

"If he don't get hurt, he's got at least 12 good years ahead," said Jake Elder, Earnhardt's crew chief.

we added wedge to tighten the car. Dale said he could live with it, and it was the only change we made all day.

"The car ran beautiful, but Dale run good, too. There's no doubt that the boy is a race driver."

Starting ninth was a bit of a disappointment for Elder and Earnhardt, but it was clear after the race started that the Osterlund Chevy was the fastest car on the high-banked, half-mile track.

Earnhardt continued to improve his position and was left with only a challenge from defending Southeastern 500 champion Waltrip after a wreck put polesitter Buddy Baker out of the race. Baker led the first 138 laps.

Baker's W.I.N. Inc., Monte Carlo collided with Cale Yarborough's Junior Johnson Olds coming out of the fourth turn on lap 210. A bent rear end housing forced Baker out of the race while Yarborough's crew made hasty repairs to the front suspension. Yarborough could complete only six more laps before having to retire.

That left the race to Earnhardt, Waltrip and Allison. Waltrip had command at first, but then a couple of fine pit stops helped turn the tide in favor of Earnhardt.

Twice he beat Waltrip down pit road. The final time, which came after a caution on lap 473, put Earnhardt in the lead to stay for the final 23 circuits. Waltrip lost ground and was passed by Allison on lap 496 and relegated to third place.

"Dale ran good, really good," said Waltrip, who was one of several top drivers to compliment Earnhardt. "He was the only one to beat, but I couldn't do it. I got a bad set of tires on the last stop and couldn't run as well as I did earlier. But give Dale credit. He did the job."

"I've received a lot of help from Bobby Allison, Richard Petty and a lot of the guys who have been racing in Grand National," said Earnhardt, the son of legendary short-track racer Ralph Earnhardt. "I sure would like to thank them for taking time to talk to me and teach me things. Thing of it is, I kinda wonder if they'll hush up now."

Earnhardt's victory not only earned him $19,800, it also put the Osterlund team on NASCAR's "Winner's Circle" program, which is designed to pay out appearance money to seven winning teams.

At a rate of $3,700 for a superspeedway race and $2,700 for a short-track event, that means the Osterlund team will net about $200,000 through the remainder of this season and all of next year.

"When we qualified ninth for this race, we didn't win tires or nothing," said Elder. "Now we can go out and buy all we need."

Richard Petty finished fourth, two laps down in his Olds. Three laps down and finishing fifth was Benny Parsons in the M.C. Anderson Monte Carlo. Donnie Allison wound up sixth in the Hoss Ellington Chevrolet. Rounding out the top 10 were rookie Terry Labonte in a Chevy, rookie Joe Millikan in a Chevy (Millikan got an object in his eye while racing and was taken to the hospital; J.D. McDuffie drove for him), James Hylton in a Chevy and Ricky Rudd in a Ford.

Earnhardt, who won with an average speed of 91.033 mph before a crowd of 26,000 led three times for 164 laps – more than any other driver.

"I really believe this is only a start," said Elder. "I think you will see the boy win some more short-track races, and I'm even looking at a couple of superspeedway wins. He's young and he's good. If he don't get hurt, he's got at least 12 good years ahead."

Twelve more years can mean many more victories for Dale Earnhardt. ∎

Rookie Grand National driver Earnhardt is just happy to find a place to sit and get ready for the race at Bristol.

Earnhardt On Top in Points

Earnhardt Surprise Winner of Atlanta 500

Dale Earnhardt wasted no time proving that his marvelous rookie season in 1979 was no fluke. He won the fifth race of the 1980 season—the Atlanta 500 at Atlanta International Raceway—for his second career victory and his first superspeedway win. Driving for Rod Osterlund, it was his fifth straight top-five finish to start the season, sending him on his way to his first NASCAR Cup championship.

Dale Earnhardt has shed his rookie stripes as smoothly as a snake sheds its skin.

The 1979 NASCAR Rookie of the Year came from a 31st starting position to win the 21st annual Atlanta 500 today at Atlanta International Raceway – his first superspeedway win and the second Grand National victory of his brief career. And the 28-year-old driver from Mooresville, N.C., continues to dominate the Winston Cup point standings with his fifth top-five finish in five starts.

The scenario didn't read so well for Earnhardt earlier in the week, however. Engine trouble during first-round qualifying prevented the team from gaining a top starting spot, and while the Osterlund Chevrolet Monte Carlo clocked the fastest time in the second session, Earnhardt's speed of 161.934 mph was still almost a full second slower than that of polesitter Buddy Baker.

"It looked bad to start with. We had problems, but we worked hard all week and overcame those problems," said Earnhardt. "I was still a little down in horsepower, but my car worked well in the corners."

Earnhardt was the fourth driver ever to win a race in his rookie year when he won the 1979 Southeastern 500 at Bristol, Tenn., a 0.533-mile track. But the win here today was particularly satisfying.

"My two favorite places are Atlanta and Charlotte, so it's good to win one here," he said. "Superspeedways are a little more prestigious and harder to win on."

The real surprise of the race was the runner-up, as the second-place money went to another 1979 Rookie of the Year – Rusty Wallace, who won that title on the USAC stock car racing circuit. Wallace, 23, was driving in his first Grand National event and his first 500-mile race ever when he brought the Penske Racing Chevrolet Caprice in nine seconds behind the Osterlund Chevy.

"I never thought that we could take a brand new car and a brand new driver and do that well. But every race I go to I try to win," said Wallace, who hopes to compete for the NASCAR Winston Cup Rookie-of-the-Year award in 1981.

"I believe if it wasn't for Donnie Allison giving me a little speech before the race I might have had problems. He told me that the car would have a tendency to break loose in the fourth turn and I needed to keep full control. He really helped me out," said Wallace. "I could make all my time in three-four."

Wallace, like Earnhardt, also had some trouble with the engine. "We had oil temperature problems. We thought the motor was bad, but the motor we put in today had the same problem. It was reading 270 degrees," he said. "That's too hot to run, but it lasted 500 miles."

Earnhardt takes the inside line and passes Cale Yarborough on his way to winning the Atlanta 500.

Earnhardt looks a little more at home in victory lane after this, his second NASCAR Grand National win.

Bobby Allison brought the Hodgdon/Curb Ford in third, and Dave Marcis, driving the Hudson Chevy Olds, finished fourth, one lap down. Dick Brooks came under his first checkered flag of the season as he finished fifth in the Sanyo Chevrolet, three laps off the pace.

Baker, who won last year's Atlanta 500 from the pole, set a new race record in qualifying Friday with a speed of 166.212 mph around the 1.522-mile speedway. The NAPA/Regal Ride Olds wasn't handling today, though, and Baker led only the first two laps before Cale Yarborough took over the front position. Baker quickly dropped out of contention.

For most of the race, Yarborough looked like a sure bet to become the first driver to win this event from a third-place start. Despite 27 lead changes among 11 drivers, the Junior Johnson-prepared Busch Chevrolet was the major force in the field, and Yarborough led 183 of the 328 laps to collect an extra $10,000 for leading the most circuits.

Seven caution periods for 45 laps allowed most of the scheduled pit stops to be staged under the yellow flag. The lead swapped hands swiftly as the frontrunners pitted, but Yarborough would soon work his way back into the front position on the restarts, stretching out to a full straightaway lead several times.

"Every race I go to I try to win," said surprise second-place finisher, Rusty Wallace.

As the race wore on, the number of cars battling behind Yarborough was gradually reduced. Richard Petty, whose STP Chevy was running particularly smooth, was sidelined after 117 laps with engine failure – his first in 35 races. Benny Parsons parked his Melling Tool Chevy three laps before the halfway mark when the clutch went out. Darrell Waltrip, running third at 192 laps, was black-flagged and sent behind the wall when the engine bearing seal broke in his Gatorade Chevy.

Donnie Allison, whose last win was here in the 1978 Dixie 500, had taken the lead on lap 169 and doggedly held off the assaults on his position. His Hawaiian Tropic Chevy was running strong, and it looked as though the Hueytown, Ala., driver might have a chance at victory.

Yarborough was right on Donnie's tail when Earnhardt and Terry Labonte hooked up and moved in on the leaders. The four edged into tight formation as they dueled for the lead. Yarborough, trying to inch past Donnie, was leading Earnhardt along the inside groove, while on the outside, Donnie was clinging tenaciously to the front spot, followed by Labonte.

Then on the 202nd lap, Labonte and Donnie tangled in the fourth turn. Hitting the outer wall, the two spun back down onto the apron, bringing out the final caution of the race. They recovered quickly and both crossed the start-finish line, Donnie from behind the pit wall, but mechanical injuries doomed their efforts.

Donnie was forced to drop out only a few laps later with a damaged rear end, a 26th place finish was all he had to show for his pains. Labonte, who broke a rotor button, lost several laps repairing the Stratagraph Chevy. He returned to the race, out of contention, to finish 15th.

Yarborough rapidly began to run away with the race on the restart. As he gained ground, Earnhardt, Bobby Allison, Wallace and Marcis shuffled positions between them.

With slightly more than 50 laps remaining, the leaders came in for their final pit stops. Yarborough took on four new tires, confident on the strength of his car to compensate for the extra time in the pits. Bobby Allison was able to assume a healthy lead.

Yarborough, running fifth, quickly moved into third behind Earnhardt. The two hooked up in a draft and started gaining on Allison. Closing in on the leader as they entered the third turn, Yarborough suddenly slowed and headed to the pits. Earnhardt continued his charge and swung past Allison as they crossed the start-finish line on lap 300.

Allison, falling back with a badly misfiring engine, was unable to challenge, and Earnhardt sailed to an easy win.

"Cale was pulling me up to Bobby, and all of a sudden Cale pulled down with ignition problems. Bobby wasn't running good at all. They both had problems," said Earnhardt, obviously not feeling overly sorry for his competitors.

With the race in the bag and 28 laps to go, Earnhardt noted that he only had one thought in his mind. "Lordy, don't have a flat tire," he recalled with a grin.

Jody Ridley was the highest finishing rookie contender with a sixth-place finish, and Baker came in seventh, both three laps in arrears. Yarborough had to settle for eighth, J.D. McDuffie was ninth and Slick Johnson came in tenth.

The race was completed in 3 hours, 42 minutes and 32 seconds at an average speed of 134.808 mph. Only 21 of the 41 starters finished the race. ■

Yarborough Fails To Rattle Sophomore

Dale Wins In Nashville

Earnhardt was able to hold off a feisty Cale Yarborough and stay ahead of Richard Petty to win his third NASCAR Grand National race of the season.

Questions about Earnhardt's toughness, mental or physical, were answered in Nashville. In a race that saw several drivers sidelined with fatigue, Earnhardt won a thrilling duel with three-time champion Cale Yarborough in the closing laps for his fourth career victory.

Dale Earnhardt was on the ropes twice in the waning laps, but the young driver from Mooresville, N.C., refused to bend on a Saturday night sizzler at Nashville Raceway.

Driving with the aplomb of a veteran of several hundred races, Earnhardt held off a furious charge by Cale Yarborough over the last 25 laps to win the 23rd annual Busch Nashville 420 by four car lengths on the 0.596-mile track.

Yarborough, who had won seven of the last 15 races here, bumped Earnhardt several times in a classic duel to the finish, but the 29-year-old sophomore driver refused to be intimidated.

Earnhardt, Yarborough and Benny Parsons had a full house of 16,700 fans on their feet for the final laps of the 250-mile race. It had been a mad dash throughout the race, but a caution flag with just 36 laps remaining set up the eventual showdown.

Bobby Allison, running on only seven cylinders since early in the race, spun out on the front straightway to bring out the only caution flag of the hot, muggy night.

Earnhardt, piloting the Osterlund Racing Chevrolet, and Yarborough changed all four tires under the caution, while Parsons took on only right side tires.

Parsons, in the M.C. Anderson/Melling Tool Chevrolet, had the lead when the race was restarted on the 389th lap. But on the backstretch on lap 391, Earnhardt and Yarborough's Busch Chevy shot by Parsons, and the latter was never a factor again.

The 29-year-old sophomore driver refused to be intimidated.

Yarborough's one major attempt to pass Earnhardt almost ended in an accident. He started around Earnhardt on the backstretch and almost bought a piece of the wall. After that, Earnhardt was in complete command, albeit Yarborough stayed within striking distance. Parsons wound up third, more than a half-lap behind in the 420-lap race.

"I didn't see him. I was the leader and I had the race track. I didn't think he would try to pass me on the outside. I know he wasn't alongside of me because I would have seen him," Earnhardt said of Yarborough's futile attempt to get by him.

Earnhardt averaged 93.811 mph in the race slowed only once for five laps. He earned $14,600 for his third win of the season and fourth of a 54-race career.

He also increased his lead to 48 points over Richard Petty in the battle for the Winston Cup championship. Petty, who required some relief driving from Harry Gant, finished fifth, four laps in arrears.

Petty came out of his car on the 347th lap. "I got cramps in my legs and had to get out," said Petty, who was fifth for the third race in a row.

Darrell Waltrip was fourth, one lap down in the DiGard Gatorade Chevrolet. He tagged Earnhardt on the 335th lap and almost spun both of them out. But they straightened their cars and kept going after the fourth-turn incident.

Six drivers called on relief. There probably would have been other calls, but only seven of the 30 starters fell out of the race. Gant was the busiest of the night. He first drove in relief of Don Sprouse after falling out, then jumped in Petty's STP Chevy.

Allison was sixth in the Bud Moore/Warner Hodgdon Ford and young Sterling Marlin was seventh in D.K. Ulrich's Waylon Jennings Chevy. Each was seven laps behind.

Yarborough led the first 150 laps. After the first series of pit stops, Parsons had a super quick tire change and took the lead on the 151st lap. Yarborough was to lead only one other lap. Parsons dominated the second third of the race, and Earnhardt was top dog in the final third, when it counted the most.

Yarborough led twice for 151 laps, Parsons set the pace four times for 137 laps, Earnhardt led three times for 103 laps, including the final 30 circuits. Petty led for 17 laps and Waltrip was in front the other two laps.

Waltrip and Petty were never seriously in contention. Petty's car wasn't running down the straights, while a long stop on lap 251 cost Waltrip a lap he wasn't to regain.

"I didn't have any close calls except there at the end with Cale. It was one of the most competitive races I've ever been in. It was a good feeling to win this one," Earnhardt said.

On the incident with Waltrip, he just grinned and said, "It was close, wasn't it?"

Asked about the stifling heat (it was 96 degrees at race time), Earnhardt said, "It was about as bad as Daytona. The hardest part was the first 100 laps. I got in the car to run 420 laps, not any less."

After what appeared to be the final pit stops, Parsons ran down Earnhardt. He was riding his bumper, ready to make a pass, when the caution flag was waved.

"I was still in front of Benny and I was prepared to stay there. After the caution, I figured it would be a race between Cale and I because we each changed four tires. I didn't think Benny could stay with us on just two new tires," Earnhardt said.

Earnhardt couldn't say enough about his crew, headed by 20-year-old Doug Richert. "Doug did a fine job in setting up the car. Doug has a lot to learn, just as I do.

But we laugh, argue a little, put our heads together and make the car go fast," he said.

He also had words of praise for engine builder Lou LaRosa. "We had a rattle in our engine Saturday, so we went to a good spare engine. Lou did a good job in making that engine run.

"We were a little loose at the beginning," Earnhardt continued, "but we added two rounds of bite and the car was handling perfectly at the end of the race.

"Goodyear also came with a harder compound, and we changed less tires than we did in May here. Goodyear is to be congratulated."

Earnhardt said his only goal this year was to win the championship, and he believes his "no name" team can do it.

"Not too many people knew any of us two years ago. But our team has it together. I'm proud of my team and I can't say enough good things about them boys," Earnhardt said. ∎

Earnhardt shares the spotlight with engine builder Lou LaRosa.

Earnhardt Wins The National 500

Dale Earnhardt Wins One For The Hometown Fans

You hear it all the time. Winning in Charlotte is a big deal not just because of the history attached to the track but because this is the place where all the teams are based. For someone like Dale Earnhardt, who grew up about 20 miles from the track, that made win No. 6 possibly the biggest in his young career. The win was his last of the season on the way to his first Cup title.

Dale Earnhardt proved today at Charlotte Motor Speedway that dreams can come true.

Ever since he was a kid growing up some 12 miles from the 1.5-mile track, Earnhardt dreamed of winning a NASCAR Grand National race there before a cheering throng of friends and neighbors.

Combining his own driving skill with that of his Osterlund Racing pit crew – led by 20-year-old Doug Richert and team manager Roland Wlodyka – Earnhardt made his dream a reality by winning the National 500.

Earnhardt and his crew won not only the race, but also almost every special incentive award that went with it. By being the quickest in the pits, the crew was given first place in the Sears Pit Crew Championship. By leading 14 times for 148 laps, including the last 47,

Earnhardt was given the Lead Foot Award. And the Osterlund team joined forces with rookie Lake Speed, who finished seventh, to win the $25,000 first prize in the much publicized Buck Stove $50,000 Team Challenge.

It was, to say the least, a near perfect day for Earnhardt, whose victory also intensified his relentless drive to the Grand National driving championship. He now has 4,217 points and is the current points leader by 115 over Cale Yarborough.

Ironically, it was Yarborough whom Earnhardt beat to the finish line by 1.83 seconds. "All of the wins are great," said the 29-year-old Earnhardt, who earned $49,050 today. "I guess I can really savor my first one [at Bristol, Tenn., in the spring of 1979] because it was my first Grand National win. But winning at Charlotte

Side-by-side with Richard Petty, Earnhardt looks like he belongs among the best.

Charlotte Motor Speedway president Bruton Smith is pleased to present the National 500 trophy to local driver, Earnhardt.

is something I have wanted to do for a long, long time. It happened in front of the hometown people, and it was something I knew I could do.

"It's got me as high or higher than I was after my win at Bristol."

The victory was Earnhardt's second in a row after his win in the Old Dominion 500 at Martinsville (Va.) Speedway last week. It was also his fifth of the season, which ties him with Darrell Waltrip for the most victories this year.

Earnhardt was helped tremendously by an excellent pit stop under green on lap 280, the last scheduled stop for the Osterlund team. Yarborough, driving the Junior Johnson Monte Carlo, was leading the race as Earnhardt took on right side tires and a tank of gas in 13.1 seconds.

Just four laps later, Yarborough pitted for 17.1 seconds and came out third, behind Buddy Baker, who trailed Earnhardt's Monte Carlo by 5.3 seconds.

Yarborough passed Baker for second place on lap 309 – just 25 circuits from the finish – and very slowly made up ground on Earnhardt. But he ran out of time.

Baker made a courageous effort to overtake Yarborough, but on the last lap, he got sideways in the fourth turn as he tried to pass on the high side. He kept the car

"Winning at Charlotte is something I have wanted to do for a long, long time." —Earnhardt

under control, dashed into pit road and across the grassy area between the road and the racing surface to cross the finish line ahead of fourth-place Ricky Rudd.

Rudd, driving his own Monte Carlo prepared under the guidance of veteran mechanic Harry Hyde, turned in his best performance of an abbreviated season.

He was given a $5,000 bonus as the top-finishing driver who had not won a Grand National race.

Donnie Allison finished fifth, followed by Bill Elliott, Speed, Jody Ridley, Kyle Petty and Dick Brooks.

"Doug Richert and Roland planned that last pit stop strategy," Earnhardt said of the fateful final stop. "They decided we would pit ahead of the other guys, and they got me in and got me out. I can drive the car as hard as it can go, but they're the guys who have to get the job done in the pits. They did."

"We just planned on getting him in and out as quickly as possible," said Richert. "We knew how far we could go on the fuel we could hold and we were pushing it to the limit, so it was a scheduled stop."

Earnhardt's plan afterward was to drive as smoothly as possible, avoid mistakes and hope that was enough to beat Yarborough, the defending National 500 champion.

"I was just going 'round and 'round, making the car do what I wanted," Earnhardt said. "I felt I had enough laps just to ride and beat him, but I wanted to make every lap count. I was contemplating what would happen if I ran too hard, messed myself up and let him have a chance to catch me. I just concentrated on running smooth, and I thought that was enough to beat him."

It was. "Yep," said Yarborough, "just say we got beat. We had some tough breaks, but we just got beat. Two things happened on my pit stop at the end. I ran out of gas and had to coast in. Then I put the gear in low, and it fell into reverse. That sounds funny, but it happened another time, too.

"After my crew made chassis adjustments on the next to last pit stop, we were really running. I was running Earnhardt down. But it was just a matter of time and we didn't have enough of it. Just say we got beat."

The pace set by most of the leaders through two-thirds of the race was hectic and, as could be expected, it took its toll. Eliminated from the competition because of wrecks were Benny Parsons (who tangled with Waltrip on lap 168 and thus lost all hope of collecting the $100,000 bonus offered him if he won the race), Neil Bonnett, Terry Labonte and Bobby Allison. Blown engines sidelined Waltrip (on lap 322) and Petty (on lap 252). A fouled ignition put David Pearson out of the race on lap 66.

For Earnhardt, who lives in Doolie, N.C., just 21 miles from the speedway, the win solidified his position as the hottest driver on the Grand National circuit. He has earned $432,675 this season, and with three races remaining, he has an excellent chance of becoming the first driver to earn $600,000 in one season.

No doubt he is aware of that. But he probably didn't think about it as he accepted the congratulations of his friends and neighbors. Foremost on his mind was the fact that, finally, he had won at Charlotte. ∎

Earnhardt Wins The Rebel 500

Earnhardt Is a Winner Again

Earnhardt snapped the first significant winless streak of his career by winning his first race at storied Darlington Raceway. Earnhardt won a thrilling duel with veteran Cale Yarborough for his first win since 1980, a span of 39 races. It also was his first win with Bud Moore Engineering. It was the first of nine career victories at Darlington for Earnhardt.

Dale Earnhardt said repeatedly that his well-publicized losing streak in NASCAR Winston Cup racing would come to an end.

It was just a matter of time.

Today at Darlington International Raceway, the time finally came.

By besting Cale Yarborough in an exciting, head-to-head duel over the final laps of the CRC Chemicals Rebel 500, Earnhardt earned his first victory since the 1980 National 500 at Charlotte Motor Speedway, 39 races ago.

It was his first win in the Bud Moore Thunderbird, which he began racing this season, and his first for Wrangler Jeans, which undertook its sponsorship at the start of the 1981 season.

More importantly for the relieved and happy Earnhardt, it put him back into the winning mold he had forged through 1979 and 1980, when he won

successively the Champion Spark Plug Rookie of the Year and Winston Cup titles.

"Wrangler and a lot of people stood by me through some hard times," said the 30-year-old Earnhardt, a resident of Doolie, N.C., a community on Lake Norman.

"I kept saying we would win and they never doubted me. They said, 'We know. You just take it easy.'"

But throughout the early part of this season, Earnhardt never took it easy – his Thunderbird was powerful enough to make him a consistent race leader. He had led every previous race this season, winning the Gillette Atra Lap Leader award for leading the most laps three times – the third being today after he paced the field 10 times for 182 circuits.

But he finished only one race, earning second place in the Valleydale 500 at Bristol Raceway. A series of mechanical problems put him out of events and, of course, away from victory lane.

Earnhardt was able to hold off Cale Yarborough to find smooth sailing to the finish line in the CRC Chemicals Rebel 500.

But he was continuously cast as a race favorite and for the CRC Chemicals Rebel 500, he lived up to the billing. He started fifth and had what his rivals admitted was the fastest car in the field.

That, however, did not make things easier. After dodging some near-disasters in the face of wrecking cars, Earnhardt had to hold off a determined challenge by Yarborough that covered the final 36 laps.

On lap 327, Kyle Petty's Pontiac smacked the fourth-turn wall on the tough 1.366-mile Darlington track and brought out the last caution of the day. Earnhardt, the leader, made his final pit stop, as did challengers Yarborough in the Valvoline Buick and Benny Parsons in the J.D. Stacy Pontiac.

Parsons was immediately put out of the competition when a cut tire forced him to the pits again, putting him nearly a lap down after running his most competitive and determined race of the year.

That left it to Yarborough and Earnhardt. Yarborough, seeking to win his second consecutive race this season, took the lead on lap 354 when he passed Earnhardt low in the third turn.

But a lap later, Earnhardt retook the lead in the first turn and never gave it up. Still, it was a nerve-crunching finish.

On the 367th and final circuit, Yarborough rode Earnhardt's rear bumper until the cars came out of the fourth turn and headed toward the finish line.

Yarborough slung his Buick low down the straightaway in an attempt to win on the widest portion of the Darlington oval. His effort almost worked. Earnhardt crossed the finish line a mere half-car length

Even after a well-documented losing streak, Earnhardt looks right at home in victory lane.

"I got beat, didn't I?" said [Cale] Yarborough. "Dale was tough."

ahead, thereby giving car owner Bud Moore his first triumph at Darlington since Darrell Dierenger won for him in the 1966 Southern 500.

"I knew Cale was gonna come to the inside," said Earnhardt, who won $31,450, including the $2,000 lap leader bonus from Gillette. "So I started to fade to the inside. I couldn't see Cale out of my left window, so I figured I had finished ahead of him."

"I got beat, didn't I?" said Yarborough. "Dale was tough. He drove a real good race and deserved to win. I had to go all out to pass Dale near the end just that one time, and he got back around me easily. So I knew it was going to be a one-shot effort to get by him.

"If I had passed him in turns one and two, he would have gotten by me in three and four. So I had to try him on four. It nearly worked. But I ran out of space."

Earnhardt's dominance of the race was obvious, as it has been before. He led 90 of the last 91 laps but the difference was that – finally – he got a dose of good luck.

"You don't ever figure you've won a race until the checkered flag falls," said Earnhardt. "Until then, Cale could have beaten me. I got some good breaks. Earlier, it seemed that Cale was able to pull up on me whenever we got into traffic. But at the end, there was no traffic and that helped."

Earnhardt also admitted luck was on his side when he avoided a few incidents that, had he been involved, could have put him out of contention.

"Bonnett hit the wall and started to come back down on me, and I didn't think I'd get through it. But then he turned back up toward the wall and that was lucky for me."

Earnhardt praised the Moore crew and said that the right tire combination enabled his Thunderbird to emerge as the race's most powerful car.

"We started the race on the tires we qualified on and took them off after our first pit stop," Earnhardt said. "We discovered that the set was the best we had and saved them until our final pit stop. We had to take only one round of bite out of the car and it ran tight all day."

Bill Elliott drove the Melling Thunderbird to a third-place finish – his best of the year – while Parsons finished fourth. Tim Richmond, driving the Stacy Buick vacated by Joe Ruttman, wound up fifth, one lap down.

Terry Labonte finished sixth in a Stacy Buick and retained his Winston Cup point lead. He now leads Parsons by 59 points (952-893).

Mark Martin finished seventh in the Apache Stove Buick, followed by Buddy Arrington in a Dodge, Donnie Allison in the Simoniz Buick, and Lennie Pond in a Buick.

Darrell Waltrip, the defending CRC Chemicals Rebel 500 champion, was eliminated after a wreck in the first turn on lap 269. He was 15 laps in arrears at the time, after an extended pit stop to correct an engine disorder that arose on lap 177.

Engine failure also claimed the cars of Richard Petty, Ron Bouchard, Dave Marcis, Jody Ridley, Morgan Shepherd, Ricky Rudd and Bobby Allison. Harry Gant finished 19th after an extended pit stop to replace a broken A-frame. He also damaged his 7-Eleven/Skoal Bandit Buick on lap 148 after hitting the fourth-turn wall.

Pole winner Buddy Baker was eliminated after just three laps with a broken flywheel.

Earnhardt won with an average speed of 123.544 mph and the race took 4 hours, 3 minutes, 27 seconds to complete. There were eight caution flags for 53 laps. ■

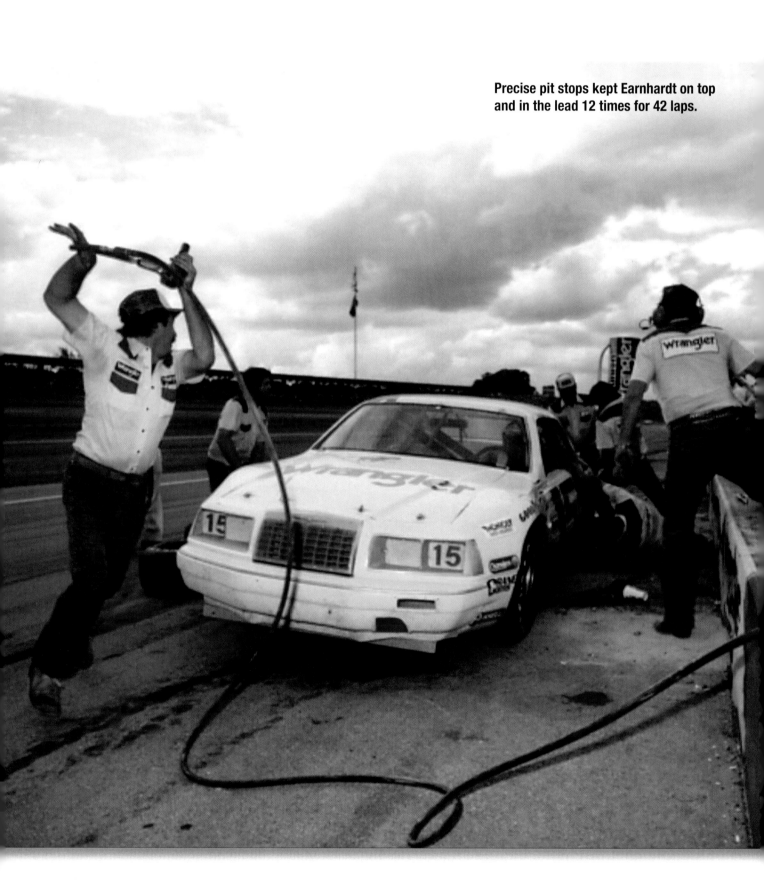

Precise pit stops kept Earnhardt on top and in the lead 12 times for 42 laps.

Last Lap Showdown

Earnhardt Tames Talladega 500

Earnhardt beat fellow driver Darrell Waltrip by half a car length with a last-lap pass to earn what would be the first of 10 career wins at Talladega. It was also his final win with car owner Bud Moore.

Dale Earnhardt made the most of the kind of opportunity he hadn't had in a long, long time.

With the aerodynamic slingshot pass that has been commonplace at the 2.66-mile Alabama International Motor Speedway, Earnhardt slipped past Darrell Waltrip on the 188th and final lap to win the Talladega 500 NASCAR Winston Cup race today.

The victory for the resident of Lake Norman, N.C., gave the race another new face – it's 14th different winner in 15 races, dating back to 1969.

More significant to Earnhardt was the fact the win was his first on a superspeedway since the 1982 Rebel (now TranSouth) 500 at Darlington, S.C.

"It was our plan to be around at the end and be in contention," said Earnhardt. "So many times in the past, we weren't able to do that. But today the car ran well all day. It was just my turn. I think we turned things around eight or nine races ago, and I'm looking forward to the rest of the 1983 season."

Driving the 1983 Bud Moore/Wrangler Ford Thunderbird, Earnhardt made his dramatic last-lap pass on Waltrip's Junior Johnson/Pepsi Challenger Chevrolet Monte Carlo down the backstretch. He then held off his Franklin, Tenn., rival to take the checkered flag by a half-car length in front of 100,000 fans and a nationwide CBS-TV audience.

Waltrip, who led four times for 21 laps, had assumed the lead on lap 178 after Neil Bonnet, driving in relief for Tim Richmond in the Old Milwaukee Pontiac, pitted for gas. Bonnett had taken over for Richmond after the latter was forced to leave the car on lap nine because a foreign substance had blown into his eye.

Earnhardt, who had pitted for the final time on lap 162, tucked into second place while Ricky Rudd's Piedmont Airlines Monte Carlo held onto third.

Ignition problems on lap 179 put Rudd out of the hunt and the race to the checkered flag was left to Waltrip and Earnhardt.

Earnhardt seemed to be in the right position, as many drivers claim the ideal spot to be in the closing laps at AIMS is second place. That permits the slingshot pass.

There was some added drama. Bobby Allison's DiGard/Miller High Life Buick ran third behind Earnhardt but was running in ninth place, two laps back after making a pit stop on lap 164 that lasted 58.8 seconds because a cracked windshield had to be replaced.

Allison, however, was in a position to assist Earnhardt by dropping behind him when the pass was made. This would theoretically propel Earnhardt's Thunderbird through the draft and by Waltrip.

"I had been studying Darrell for a long time, trying to determine where I could make the pass," said Earnhardt. "As we came out of the second turn and onto the backstretch, I saw the slower cars of Bobby Hillin and Kyle Petty ahead. I figured they'd be a factor as we got into the trioval so I thought I would go ahead and pass."

As he did, Allison joined him to the inside of Waltrip's Monte Carlo. "Darrell then did just what I would've done," said Earnhardt. "He tried to take up as much of the track as he could and sort of pushed me and Bobby to the infield. That was his option."

Earnhardt took the lead in the third turn and as he came out of the fourth turn and into the trioval, Allison dropped low to the inside out of the way. Waltrip still had an opportunity to make a pass of his own.

"I don't know if Bobby had helped me or not," said Earnhardt. "That's a big 'if.' I'm not sure I could've gotten completely around Darrell when I did without Bobby, but I do feel confident I could have drafted around him at any rate.

"I knew that when we got to the trioval Darrell was going to try and pass me. I just didn't know which direction he'd take. I was picking up on him pretty good because I was drafting on Hillin's car. Just as I came up on it I cut to the outside. I had plenty of room there.

"As I crossed the finish line, I looked over and saw Hillin's car but not Darrell's. I was tickled to death."

Waltrip, who was gunning for a second straight Talladega 500 win – he is the only man to win the race twice – claimed he had let Earnhardt pass.

"I let Dale get around me because I figured I could get back around him going into the trioval," said the defending Winston Cup champion. "But then we ran up on a slower car and that won the race for Dale. I'm thankful for that second-place finish, however. It helped us gain some ground in the point standings."

Waltrip now lurks in second place in the standings behind Allison with 2,782 points. Allison has 2,947 points with 11 races remaining in 1983.

Bonnett drove Richmond's car to a third-place finish while Richard Petty took fourth in the STP Pontiac. Harry Gant's Skoal Bandit Buick nipped Geoff Bodine's Gatorade Pontiac for fifth place, while Dick Brooks finished seventh in the Donlavey/Chameleon Sunglasses Thunderbird, one lap down. Taking positions eight through 10 were Bill Elliott in the Melling Oil Pumps Thunderbird, Allison and Mark Martin in the Jim McGill Monte Carlo.

Bonnett was available as a relief driver because his Hodgdon/Rahmoc Monte Carlo blew an engine after the first lap. That triggered the day's only accident, which involved eight cars and sidelined five.

"As I crossed the finish line, I looked over and saw Hillin's car but not Darrell's. I was tickled to death." —Earnhardt

Eliminated were the cars of Grant Adcox, Dick Skillen, Travis Tiller, Billie Harvey and Tommy Gale.

"My motor blew going into the third turn," explained Bonnett. "It just exploded, driving the crankshaft through the engine. My oil got all over the place and that's when everybody started spinning in the fourth turn."

Skillen's car plowed into the outside wall, while Adcox's was demolished when it collided with the inside wall and then was hit by other cars.

Terry Labonte left the race after 66 laps when the engine in his Hagan/Budweiser Monte Carlo blew, bringing out the only other caution of the day. The two cautions for just 16 laps allowed Earnhardt to win with an average speed of 170.611 mph, the second-fastest Talladega 500 ever. Lennie Pond won in 1978 with a speed of 174.700 mph.

Earnhardt's win – his second of the year – meant that Fords have now won three of the last four Winston Cup events. Prior to the streak, Ford's last win came in the 1982 World 600 at Charlotte, N.C., when Neil Bonnett drove a Wood Brothers Thunderbird.

There were 46 lead changes among ten drivers, with Earnhardt earning the Gillette-Atra Lap Leader Award by leading 12 times for 41 laps.

Pole winner Cale Yarborough left the race after 140 laps, the victim of a blown engine in his Ranier/Hardee's Monte Carlo. Buddy Baker, who led six times for 30 laps, retired on lap 69 after his brakes went out. David Pearson and Lake Speed also suffered engine failure, as did Benny Parsons. Twenty-one of the 40 cars that started the 2-hour, 55-minute, 52-second race were running at the finish. ■

After edging rival Darrell Waltrip during an exhilarating last lap, Earnhardt can smile and breathe a sigh of satisfaction, knowing he is back on track to win more races.

Earnhardt Survives At Bristol

Earnhardt "Muscles" Way To Victory

Drivers typically have to manhandle their cars around Bristol—and that's with power steering. Losing his power steering just 100 laps into the 500-lap race, Earnhardt earned possibly the toughest win of his career to date in a race where 20 drivers were involved in accidents. He led seven times for 213 laps, taking the lead on lap 483 after a three-lap, side-by-side, sheet-metal-rubbing battle with Ricky Rudd.

Dale Earnhardt lived up to his reputation as a rugged, no-quarter-given race driver today as he manhandled a car which had lost its power steering to victory in the Valleydale 500 NASCAR Winston Cup race at Bristol International Raceway.

With 100 laps gone in the 500-lap event, Earnhardt's Childress/Wrangler Chevrolet Monte Carlo changed from a quick-steering, smooth-handling speedster into an uncooperative brute. However, it handled well enough for Earnhardt's strength to force it into the lead seven times for 213 laps.

But only after a critical pit stop during the day's 15th caution period (a record at BIR) was Earnhardt able to get the measure of Moore/Motorcraft Ford Thunderbird driver Ricky Rudd and take the victory by 1.14 seconds.

With the win, Earnhardt joined Bill Elliott as the only drivers to win twice this year. Earnhardt has claimed victory at the only two short-track events run so far this season, having also won the Feb. 24 Miller High Life 400 at Richmond, Va., before winning on the 0.533-mile Bristol track for the third time in his career.

There can be little doubt that today's win was his toughest ever.

"I've never driven a car which had lost the power steering, and I hope I never do it again," said Earnhardt, a resident of Doolie, N.C., on the shores of Lake Norman. "It was like having someone in the car holding the wheel, trying to keep you from turning it. You had to fight all the time.

"Drove the last 400 laps without the power steering. I don't know what happened but, fortunately, the whole thing didn't give out. I had to pull on the wheel so much my right hand and arm went to sleep. When I could, I tried to steer with one hand so I could work my right arm and try to get it to recover a bit."

Earnhardt added that only the superior handling of the car allowed him to finish.

"If the car hadn't handled so good, even with the power steering gone, I would have never finished the race. But it did get to hurting me so bad that I radioed (team owner Richard Childress) and told him to go find someone just in case I gave out or something," he said.

Darrell Waltrip, knocked out of the race because of a blown engine in his Johnson/Budweiser Monte Carlo, stood by to drive relief but was never utilized.

"We decided to play it lap by lap," said Earnhardt, who won $31,525 for his 13th career victory. "I got a break because of all the cautions, but it got tough even with them after a while."

Earnhardt and Ricky Rudd rubbed and scraped through the final three laps.

The race was characterized by yellow flags. The 15 that flew bettered the old Bristol record of 12 set last spring and was just two short of the modern day NASCAR record of 17 set in the Old Dominion 500 of 1980 at Martinsville (Va.) Speedway.

It reached the point where most of the cars in the field looked like refugees from a junkyard. Many drivers were involved in more than one incident and by just the 55th lap, eight of the more competitive cars were either laps in arrears or out of the event completely. More would follow.

Earnhardt escaped the carnage, even though his power steering had given out.

"I reckon there were just a wild and crazy bunch of guys out there," he said. "You had to pay attention. I started 12th and right away I started worrying about what might happen ahead of me. Sure enough, we hadn't gone far (eight laps, to be exact) before Lake Speed and a bunch of others got into it and started tearing things up. It was senseless that it happened that early and it involved a lot of good cars.

"I guess it was one of those days at Bristol. It's an exciting place to race and it's exciting for the fans to watch. But they work us to death here putting on the show."

Earnhardt added he had his share of close calls as the race wore on. On lap 362 he lost his lead to Rudd after he rubbed a slower car while passing in the third turn.

"That one got me sideways and I locked it up," Earnhardt said. "With the power steering out, I have no idea how the car got straight again, but it did."

Rudd maintained his lead as Earnhardt gave chase. Try as he might, however, it appeared that Earnhardt had only the slightest chance of catching his Thunderbird-driving rival, who was gunning for his first victory of the 1985 season.

"I had a tire problem," said Earnhardt. "I had blistered the left rear tire and the car was working as well off the corners as it could have. I got some good laps in on Ricky, but in the traffic he could pull away. If it had kept on that way, I think he would have beaten me. He was awful strong."

The Earnhardts, once again, grace victory lane.

But fate gave Earnhardt the chance he needed. On lap 477, the day's final yellow flag flew when rookie Don Hume spun in the second turn. Earnhardt seized the opportunity to take on much-needed left-side tires. Rudd pitted for right-side rubber.

When the green flag came out on lap 480, Rudd and Earnhardt began racing side by side, rubbing metal at least a half-dozen times before Earnhardt's blue-and-yellow Monte Carlo took the lead on the frontstretch on lap 483.

"We were lucky," said Earnhardt, "because we had changed right-side tires on our last stop and planned to change the left-side tires when we made that final stop. As it happened, that is exactly what we needed. I know I got into Ricky but, with the power steering gone, I needed more lanes out there."

"Bud (Moore, team owner and crew chief) wanted to change left-side tires but I wanted the right-sides," said Rudd, "and I guess that was a bad decision. It made us run a little too tight and the car was pushing. After the tire change, there was no way I could run with him. If I could have kept Dale on hot tires, I could have run even or ahead of him.

"But this was a good finish and a good lift for the team." Rudd led twice for 163 laps and won $18,050 for his runner-up finish.

By lap 204, well under the halfway point of the race, 10 caution flags had flown. It was so hectic that, prior to that, the longest stretch run under green had been 49 laps. For the race, the longest green-flag period was 80 laps. Several drivers were involved in more than one accident, among them Neil Bonnett (eventually knocked out on lap 137 after clobbering the frontstretch pit wall), Harry Gant (who limped home 20th), Bill Elliott (who wound up 11th, 15 laps down), Lake Speed (who was seventh, five laps down) and Waltrip, the 23rd-place finisher. In all, 20 different cars were involved in accidents.

"Overall, I was driving pretty cautious, but I was lucky to get by it all," said Earnhardt. "I was, as I said, concerned about starting back there in 12th place. We had missed it in qualifying (March 30). I scuffed up some tires for it, but we thought new ones would be the way to go so that is what we did. But that messed us up. We should have started fourth or fifth, we were lucky to get through it all."

Earnhardt, who won with an average speed of just 81.790 mph, said that some intense preparation on the part of his team for the short tracks benefited him today.

"During the winter, Kirk (Shelmerdine, crew chief) and I worked hard on the setups," he said. "Last year we were torn on it with power steering and setting caster and camber, stuff like that. We changed a lot during the season. But then, for this year, we worked on the basics, going about getting the settings we'd use all year. It seems to have worked for us.

"Like I said, it was very, very tough without power steering but, if the car hadn't handled the way it did, it would have been much worse."

Terry Labonte finished third, two laps down in the Hagan/Piedmont Airlines Monte Carlo, and assumed the Winston Cup points lead. He is the fifth different leader through the first five events of the season. He was involved in the first incident of the day (along with four other cars), and lost his laps when he took a two-lap penalty to change all four flat-spotted tires during a caution period. The penalty is enforced under the NASCAR rule which permits only two-tire changes during the yellow flag. A four-tire change brings a two-lap penalty.

Buddy Baker finished fourth, also two laps down, in the Bull Frog/Liquid Wrench Oldsmobile, a fine showing for the driver, who does not favor the short tracks. Rusty Wallace was fifth in the Stewart/AluGard Pontiac, three laps back, while Kyle Petty took sixth in the Wood Brothers/7-Eleven Thunderbird, five laps down.

Speed was seventh, followed by Richard Petty, Bobby Hillin and rookie Ken Schrader.

The race, which was run after a six-day postponement following rain on March 31, took three hours, 15 inutes and 30 seconds to complete.

Earnhardt's arms and back, however, are expected to be sore for a considerably longer time. ■

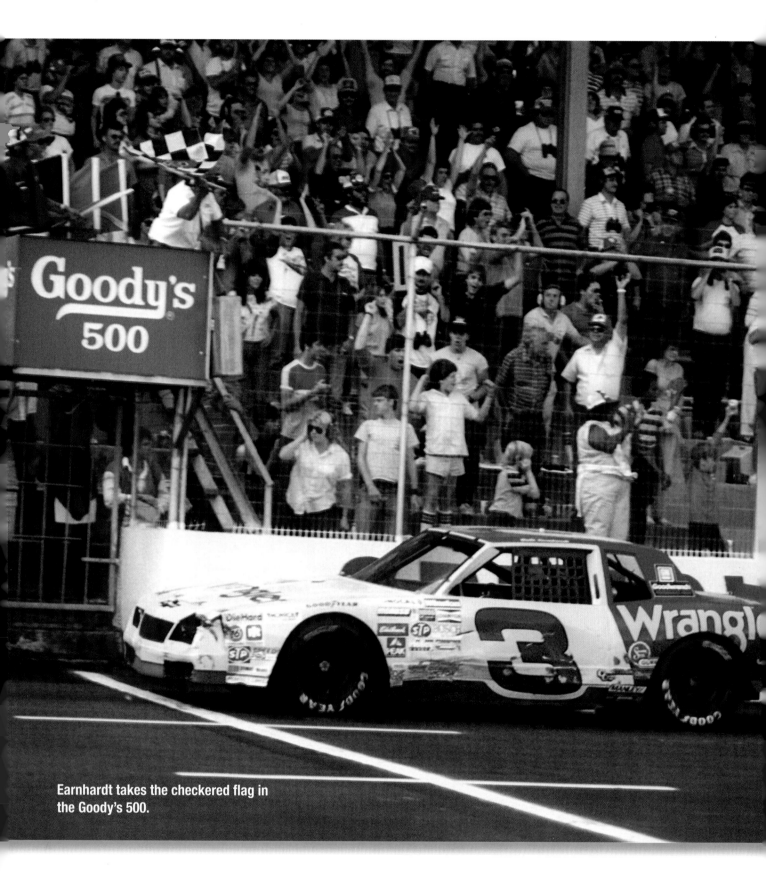

Earnhardt takes the checkered flag in
the Goody's 500.

Battered, But Not Beaten, Is Earnhardt at Martinsville

Earnhardt's "Touch" Is A Winner

Dale Earnhardt scored his second career victory at Martinsville Speedway in what became typical Earnhardt style. He bumped and banged his way past Tim Richmond and Darrell Waltrip in the final laps to win the Goody's 500, drawing the ire of both drivers and starting heated rivalries that would last for years to come. "They can't continue to allow him to do it," Richmond said. "That's Martinsville, I guess," Earnhardt said.

Dale Earnhardt used the years of experience he gained running on the dirt and asphalt "bullrings" of the Carolinas to pull a gutsy move that resulted in his winning today's Goody's 500 NASCAR Winston Cup event at Martinsville Speedway.

In a typical Martinsville race that several competitors called "physical," Earnhardt, driving the Childress/Wrangler Chevrolet Monte Carlo, bullied his way alongside the Blue Max/Old Milwaukee Pontiac of race leader Tim Richmond coming out of the fourth turn on the 443rd lap. Richmond tried hard to keep the lead; the duo swept down toward the pit road wall on the front straightaway and as they entered the first corner they were still battling fiercely for the No. 1 position.

Just then, Greg Sacks' DiGard/Miller American Buick made contact with the Coors/Melling Ford Thunderbird of Bill Elliott and Elliott spun out in the second turn. Earnhardt, in avoiding Elliott, darted to the inside, took the lead going into the backstretch and kept it from there on out.

Richmond, who had led twice for 159 laps (the most of anyone) later experienced troubles on a pit stop when a lug nut got behind a wheel and jammed the brake rotor. He had already changed two tires, had to pit again for another fresh right-front tire when the wheel froze up, thereby violating the NASCAR rule stating no more than two tires may be changed on a yellow-flag pit stop and he ended up finishing seventh, two laps off the pace.

The race's defending champion, Darrell Waltrip, then took over second place and began to dog Earnhardt. On lap 453, his Johnson/Budweiser Monte Carlo and Earnhardt's car made contact in the first corner as the two fought for supremacy.

By lap 478, Earnhardt was almost two seconds in front of Waltrip. He stretched his advantage to 2.6 seconds by lap 481 and by the time the 489th of 500 circuits around the 0.526-mile flat track had been completed the Wrangler driver's advantage over Waltrip was 3.2 seconds.

The last of a dozen yellow flags for 65 laps came out on lap 494 when Bobby Hillin spun his Trap Rock Industries Monte Carlo out in the third corner. Both Waltrip and Harry Gant, who was running third in the Skoal Bandit Monte Carlo (and the last car on the lead lap), pitted for left-side tires while Earnhardt did not.

The green flag was waved for the last time on lap 497 and Gant ducked back into his pit for right-side rubber, going a lap down. Waltrip made one last attempt to pass Earnhardt in the third turn on the next lap, but it was to no avail and he finished two car lengths behind the winner.

Gant finished third. Fourth, and a lap down, was Ricky Rudd in the Moore/Motorcraft Thunderbird, while Kyle Petty took fifth in the Wood Brothers/7-Eleven Thunderbird, two laps off the pace.

"That was a pretty close call on that last stop. To get tires or not to get tires," said Earnhardt of his decision not to pit. "If I had pitted first, Darrell wouldn't have.

"I hadn't got the caution flag yet and I had a lap to think about it. It was a gamble and when Richard (car owner Childress) asked, 'What do you want to do?' I said, 'Let's go for it!'"

Earnhardt explained that when new tires are put on a car, "They're good, but not as good as they're going to be." It takes a few laps for them to effect maximum gripping power and had the caution come earlier or the race run longer, Waltrip and perhaps even Gant may have been able to pass him.

In fact, when the final caution flag flew, Earnhardt, who has now won four races this year (all on short tracks), admitted to being startled.

"Oh s---, what am I going to do now? Am I going to pit? My mind was going yes and no, yes and no," said Earnhardt. "And when Darrell pitted that decided it. I was going to gamble."

Thirty-one cars started the 263-mile race and 21 finished. Eight of the 12 cautions were for wrecks or spinouts.

The "one-groove" track took its toll on sheet metal and suspension parts and just after the checkered flag fell, Richmond was prompted to accuse Earnhardt of rough driving. That was something the race winner denied.

"He pulled the same stunt again. We ain't even yet," said Richmond, alluding to the fact that for the third time this year he was a victim of Earnhardt's driving style on the short tracks on which Earnhardt had won.

"We've got a long way to go. (But) he can get away with it as long as it sells tickets, I guess." "They can't allow him to continue to do it," said Richmond.

Waltrip was more subdued, saying, "I don't want to get into that." But when asked when competitiveness ended and overly-aggressive driving took over, he said, "You just witnessed it."

Earnhardt admitted to making contact with Richmond but said it wasn't intentional. He noted that metal-to-metal contact is required at Martinsville because of the track's configuration and added that he had driven carefully most of the way in order to conserve his car for the final late-race charge.

"I bumped him a little in the corner and he backed off a little bit," said Earnhardt. "He gave me a shot and let me know he didn't like it.

"That's Martinsville, I guess, and I must have gotten hit 100 times. At Martinsville you've got to run 500 laps and brakes are key to being competitive.

"I ran conservative, and when 60 laps to go came, it was time to go," said Earnhardt. "We pitted that time (on the 11th caution) and got lefts. Darrell got rights and I think that was the key to the win."

However, the event was something of a barnburner in style not found on the superspeedways. Pole winner Geoff Bodine shot into the lead and led the first 62 laps in the Hendrick/Levi Garrett Monte Carlo. He kept the front spot until the first yellow flag on lap 62. He came back to lead laps 64–119, 121–129 and 175–202 but dropped out at 288 laps with engine failure.

Choosing an inside line, Earnhardt blows past rival and friend Neil Bonnett.

"He pulled the same stunt again.
We ain't even yet." —Tim Richmond

Morgan Shepherd and Ron Bouchard each led a single lap. Gant went to the front once for five laps. Waltrip paced the field twice for 121 laps and Earnhardt led the final 58.

The caution flag came out twice because of debris on the track, two more times due to blown engines, five more times because of single- or multi-car spinouts and three additional times for accidents.

The worst – and one that further tightened the points between Waltrip and Elliott for the Winston Cup crown – occurred between turns one and two on lap 342 when Waltrip and Elliott, along with Rudd, Richard Petty, Kyle Petty and Bouchard all either piled into each other or the wall.

Waltrip ended up on the infield grass, Elliott came to rest against the wall, and Petty's car was too badly damaged to continue on. Waltrip was the luckiest, with no serious damage to his Monte Carlo. Bouchard's Buick was mangled, but he kept going and completed 498 laps to finish sixth, while Elliott had to go behind the wall. Among other things, the steering linkage on his car was completely broken.

Elliott reentered the race on lap 365 but was black-flagged three laps later. The toe-in on his car was off kilter and could have caused a tire to blow, thus possibly precipitating another accident.

He rejoined the event on lap 372 but could muster only a 17th-place finish, 33 laps down. While he still leads in points, the deficit between him and Waltrip was whittled down to 23 points, 3,523 to 3,500.

"It was a very tough race. This is a hard track to pass on," said Waltrip. "We had some trouble up there in turn two.

"Somebody hit me and I don't know who it was. I was lucky to get out of it.

"That's more important than anything. We're going to win that championship," he added when told that he was that much closer to Elliott.

And for Earnhardt's goals for the year? It's tough to bounce back from early and mid-season misfortunes, win more races and complete the season with a top-10 points finish. He is not in the chase to the championship.

"We ran a good, smooth, conservative race and saved the car to the end," said Earnhardt. "I think Darrell and Harry did, too.

"Darrell is a tough person to beat here, or Tim, or Harry, or any of them. And when they got tires at the end, I knew it would be tough as hell to beat them.

"(The goal) is to try and win more races and get back in the top 10 in points," he said.

By finishing eighth, five laps back, in the Trap Rock Industries Monte Carlo, Bobby Hillin Jr., posted his third top-10 finish of the year. Neil Bonnett was ninth, also five laps down, in the Johnson/Budweiser Monte Carlo and Bobby Allison completed 494 laps to finish 10th in his own Miller American Buick.

The victory was Earnhardt's second at Martinsville, ninth on a track of less than a mile in length and 15th overall, tying him with Bonnett for 25th place on the all-time win list. He completed the race in three hours, 43 minutes and 13 seconds at an average speed of 70.694 mph and won $37,725 in front of a crowd estimated at 37,000 – a record for the Goody's 500. ■

No. 3 Wins No. 3 Of The Season

Earnhardt Toughest When It Counted

It took him seven years, but Earnhardt finally conquered the series' longest race by patiently saving his equipment and overtaking Bill Elliott with just 16 laps remaining at Charlotte Motor Speedway. Finally winning the grueling 600, he said, was "a dream come true."

Dale Earnhardt usually wins races by attacking a speedway like a bull. But, in the Coca-Cola 600 at Charlotte Motor Speedway, he was more like a crafty fox.

Playing a sly waiting game with Coors/Melling Ford Thunderbird driver Bill Elliott, Earnhardt took the lead when Elliott had to pit for needed gasoline just 16 laps from the finish and then brought his Childress/Wrangler Chevrolet Monte Carlo SS home 1.59 seconds ahead of Tim Richmond in the Hendrick/Folgers Chevrolet.

It was the first Coca-Cola 600 victory of Earnhardt's career and his third of the season, as the Doolie, N.C., resident also won at Darlington, S.C., and North Wilkesboro, N.C., in April. He is the winningest NASCAR Winston Cup driver of the season to date.

But, it did not come easily on the 1.5-mile CMS track, Earnhardt's "home" speedway. Although he was one of a record 15 drivers to swap the lead 38 times, his presence wasn't felt until after his final pit stop on lap 336, when the leaders began a series of green-flag stops.

When they were completed, Earnhardt was 1.96 seconds behind Elliott – but there were a couple of significant differences. Earnhardt's Chevrolet had finally attained the balance of wedge and tire stagger his team had been seeking all day to improve its handling and everyone present knew that Elliott would have to stop for fuel one more time.

Because Elliott's Ford simply could not achieve the gas mileage afforded Earnhardt's Chevrolet, a final pit stop was inevitable. Elliott's only hope was that he could do it under caution.

But that was not to be. Therefore, all Earnhardt had to do was pace himself behind his rival and move into the lead when the opportunity arose.

"We made a good stop the last time," said Earnhardt, who earned $98,150 for his victory. "We filled the car up with gas and we knew that Bill had to make one more stop. Still, I kept the car loaded and ready. I wasn't playing with Bill, but I was content to run behind him.

Second place finisher and regular track rival Tim Richmond congratulates Earnhardt on his third Winston Cup win of the season.

"I didn't pressure the car. I was saving it and the tires and I felt I had enough left to get by Bill at the end if I had to."

By lap 349, Earnhardt had caught Elliott and rode his bumper until lap 384, when Elliott made the pit stop he had to make. He spent just 4.15 seconds off the track for a splash of fuel, but it sent him into fifth place, some 18 seconds behind Earnhardt.

"We just had to stop for fuel," said Elliott, who was seeking his first Winston Cup win of the season. "If we hadn't we would have been out of gas and we ran out twice in the race as it was. Our problem was that we kept the burned piston from the Talladega race (the May 4 Winston 500) in our mind and we jetted the engine a little richer than we usually would for here. We sacrificed a little horsepower for a little more conservative engine, which we hoped would run all the way.

"We needed a yellow flag there in the last 30 laps or so and I think we would have made life VERY interesting for those who finished the race ahead of us at the end."

After taking the lead from Elliott, Earnhardt's only task was to be wary of Richmond, who lurked less than two seconds behind. But Richmond, who started from the No. 2 position, couldn't make up any ground and ended up holding off Cale Yarborough in the Ranier/Hardee's Ford in a furious battle for the runner-up position, which Richmond won by a hood length.

"I knew he was there," said Earnhardt of Richmond. "I kept radioing back to the pits to find out his position. I felt I had enough to put the pressure on if he hooked up with someone and caught up with me."

"The track came to Dale at the end and I had to keep the rear end of my car hung out," said Richmond. "It wasn't the first time I've had one taken away from me here. I would have liked to have won."

Despite not winning, Richmond was one of the day's dominant drivers. He joined Harry Gant in the Skoal Bandit Chevrolet, Yarborough and Elliott as a potent front-runner. Each sped away from the remainder of the field during intervals of the race and, combined, they led 340 of 400 laps.

Earnhardt was not among them, leading just twice for 26 laps, including the all-important final 16.

"It was so important to get the right tire combinations and stagger here," he said. "The wedge (weight on either side of the car) and tires have to work together.

"I didn't feel at the start of the race that we had a shot at winning. We were running a higher gear than anyone else and I wasn't sure that's what we should have done. It was a decision between me and Richard (Childress, team owner).

"Halfway through the race, I still wasn't happy. But Kirk (Shelmerdine, crew chief) and Richard kept working with the stagger and wedge and, with about 100 laps to go, I found the groove I needed.

"The track came to me, so to speak. The higher gear went to work. I could run high on the track and get the RPMs I needed. That's where I beat the others. They got loose in the corners and while I didn't beat them going in, by the time I got to the middle I got the power I needed."

Rainfall in the first and second turns brought out the day's sixth and final caution period on laps 267 to 276. Before the yellow flag, leader Yarborough and runner-up Richmond had built a commanding 10-second lead on the field and were in a position to put Earnhardt a lap down, since the eventual winner was no more than a half-straightaway ahead.

But the caution changed things. Elliott pitted early while Yarborough and Richmond opted for a four-tire change just two laps before the green flag flew. As a result, Elliott was in command for the next 54 laps. When he pitted on lap 327, Earnhardt took over for 10 laps, then pitted, giving Richmond the lead for two laps. Then Darrell Waltrip in the Johnson/Budweiser Chevrolet, led for one lap. The lead passed to Gant for a lap before Elliott took over for 44 more laps, giving the lead – and the win – to Earnhardt with 16 laps remaining.

The win was especially pleasing to Earnhardt, the son of former dirt-track and Late Model Sportsman great Ralph Earnhardt, who passed away in 1974.

"I can remember standing on a flatbed truck in the infield watching this race with my daddy," said Earnhardt, the 1979 NASCAR rookie of the year and 1980 Winston Cup champion. "I told him, 'Maybe someday you will win here,' and I always have wished that he could have raced here with a competitive car because I think he could have won.

"But it was my dream to win here. I won the National 500 in 1980, and that was good but it wasn't the 600. Now that I have won, it is my dream come true."

Earnhardt, who now has 18 career victories and whose previous high finish in the Coca-Cola 600 was second to Bobby Allison in 1984, padded his Winston Cup points lead over Waltrip. He now has 1,767 points, 144 more than Waltrip, who has 1,623.

"It is a long way to the end of the season," said the 35-year-old Earnhardt. "Every race counts. We're fortunate in that we've been able to pick up bonus points for leading in every race and we've had good finishes. It's our goal to win races and win the championship for Richard Childress and his team."

Going into the Coca-Cola 600, two drivers, Allison and Geoff Bodine, were looking for victory and a $100,000 bonus from R.J.R. Nabisco in its Winston Million program. The program awards the cash to any driver who can win two of the four selected events and $1 million to the competitor who wins three of them. The events are the Daytona 500, the Winston 500, the Coca-Cola 600 and the Southern 500. Bodine won the Daytona 500, and Allison the Winston 500. However, Bodine fell out of the Coca-Cola 600 with a broken camshaft after 319 laps to finish 31st and Allison came home 12th, two laps down.

With his win at Charlotte, Earnhardt becomes the third candidate for the $100,000 bonus when the Winston Cup series rolls into Darlington, S.C., for the Aug. 31 Southern 500.

Behind Earnhardt, Richmond and Yarborough came fourth-place Gant. Waltrip finished fifth with Elliott, who was the last driver to complete all 400 laps, sixth. Seventh place went to Sterling Marlin in the Ellington/ Bull's Eye Chevrolet. Ricky Rudd took eighth in the Moore/Motorcraft Ford. Morgan Shepherd was ninth in the Race Hill Farm Buick LeSabre and Rusty Wallace

**"Now that I have won, it is my dream come true."
—Earnhardt, on winning the 600**

Car owner Richard Childress and Earnhardt share the spotlight and the success.

rounded out the top ten in the Blue Max/AluGard Pontiac Grand Prix 2+2.

Thirty-one of the field's 41 starters were running at the finish. Among those who fell out were David Pearson because of overheating and Benny Parsons, a victim of a broken shock mount. Greg Sacks retired after an accident and engine failure eliminated Richard Petty. Petty, whose STP Pontiac was rendered useless after an accident in practice on May 23 that gave him a

concussion and kept him in a hospital overnight, drove D.K. Ulrich's Chevrolet and left after 123 laps. He finished 38th.

Next for the Winston Cup competitors is the June 1 Budweiser 400 at the 2.62-mile Riverside, Calif., road course. "We're going out there loaded for bear," said Earnhardt.

He was loaded in the Coca-Cola 600, also – when it counted. ■

Earnhardt emerged from his Wrangler Chevrolet the race winner in Atlanta, a two-time Winston Cup champion and $833,950 richer.

The Year Belongs To Earnhardt

Earnhardt Romp$ And A eaon I$ Won

With a 144-point lead on Darrell Waltrip and just two races left, Earnhardt didn't need to win this race to put himself in position to win the title. When Waltrip's engine died just 83 laps into the event, Earnhardt didn't need to win this race to even clinch the title. But win he did. He lapped the entire field on the way to victory and clinching the 1986 title—his first driving for Richard Childress—with one race still left in the season.

It was there for Dale Earnhardt's taking and take it he did – by the bushel.

Just about every major post-season award available in NASCAR Winston Cup racing fell into Earnhardt's hands after his imposing victory in the Atlanta Journal 500 at Atlanta International Raceway.

Unquestionably, the most significant of these was the 1986 Winston Cup championship, which Earnhardt officially clinched on lap 303 of the 328-lap race on the 1.522-mile AIR track. Entering the race with a lead of 144 points over rival Darrell Waltrip, Earnhardt was presented a golden opportunity to end the title war when the engine in Waltrip's Johnson/Budweiser Chevrolet Monte Carlo SS expired after just 83 laps.

Earnhardt seized his chance with a vengeance. In his typical style, which has been called everything from "aggressive" to "crazy," Earnhardt put his Childress/Wrangler Chevrolet at the point four times for 162 laps and mauled the field, finishing one lap and three seconds ahead of Richard Petty in the STP Pontiac Grand Prix 2+2. In doing so, Earnhardt established a track record average speed for a 500-mile race at AIR, coming home at 152.523 mph and bettering the old mark of 144.925 mph set by Benny Parsons in March of 1984.

With the convincing victory, Earnhardt became the first driver to clinch a Winston Cup championship before the last race of the season, the Winston Western 500 at Riverside, Calif., since 1978. In October of that year, Cale Yarborough won the Nationwise 500 at North Carolina Motor Speedway and thereby locked up the title by 424 points over Bobby Allison with two races remaining. Earnhardt now goes to Riverside with an unbeatable 278-point pad over Waltrip (4,293-4,015). The margin is so great Earnhardt could choose not to enter that West Coast race and still retain the championship.

But, there's more.

Including the $67,000 he earned for winning the race, the bonus money from clinching both the Stewart Warner miles leader and True Value Hardware lap leader awards and the $716,000 in various contingency awards he will be presented for his championship, Earnhardt had an astonishing payday of $833,950.

It was Earnhardt's second championship and the first for his Winston-Salem, N.C., team owned by former "independent" driver Richard Childress. In 1980, while driving for Rod Osterlund in only his second full year on the Winston Cup circuit, Earnhardt won his first title.

"How could it have been more perfect?" said Earnhardt of his day. "Maybe if I had won the pole (taken by Dawsonville, Ga.'s Bill Elliott at a track record 172.905 mph), but then the Georgia fans wouldn't have liked it.

"Yes, it was bittersweet to see Darrell go out. It is always better, always more exciting to race for the championship. Darrell and Junior Johnson have been strong for several years, but Richard Childress and his team worked hard all year long. This year, I think they did the better job. Me, I just tried to do my part and it is the team that deserves all the praise for this championship.

"It was Richard's effort that built the team and put it in the position it is in today. Anytime you run an entire season without a lot of loose ends to tie, you have confidence and you know you are going to do well."

No one thought Earnhardt would not do well at Atlanta, but there was some question about a victory, particularly as the early stages of the race developed.

At that time, the race belonged to Harry Gant. Driving the Skoal Bandit Chevrolet and looking for his first win of the 1986 season, Gant took the lead on lap 67 when Waltrip pitted under the green. Gant was not obliged to follow since he had made a stop under the day's first caution period on lap 18. That proved to be beneficial because it put him out of synch with the remainder of the field, which was constantly having to make green-flag stops since the race experienced only two caution flags for seven laps.

By the halfway point of the race, Gant had pushed his margin to nearly six seconds over second-place Tim Richmond in the Hendrick/Folgers Chevrolet, while Earnhardt ran third.

But Gant lost his advantage on lap 189, when Alan Kulwicki spun his Quincy's Ford Thunderbird in the fourth turn to bring out the second caution. Gant was forced to pit with the other leaders but came out in second place behind Earnhardt when the race resumed on lap 194. From that point until the checkered flag, it was all Earnhardt. He continuously expanded his lead over Gant and third-place runner Morgan Shepherd in the Rahmoc/Nationwise Pontiac. Then the end came prematurely for both of his rivals.

Gant had begun backing up with a dropped cylinder and was forced to retire with engine failure on lap 285. Shepherd followed two laps later with the same malady. Therefore, the question was not would Earnhardt win but, rather, by how much. It was answered quickly. He led 135 of the final 138 laps.

"We were really whistlin' there for a while," said Gant. "We lost a cylinder and finally it blew. I actually warped a valve and she just blew."

"At the first of the race, Tim and Harry were running better than I was," said Earnhardt, a 35-year-old resident of Doolie, N.C. "On those green-flag stops we all had to make, Harry had us beat, but then things turned around when we got that second caution. It enabled us to change tires and get the right stagger on our car, which then became the car to beat."

It was on the 303rd lap that Earnhardt became the champion because, at that point, the worst disaster would have relegated him to 26th place – still good enough to beat Waltrip, who finished 39th, for the title.

"No, they didn't tell me on the radio that I had won the title," said Earnhardt, who won for the fifth time this

Dale shares his second points championship with his mother, Martha.

"When you go out to kick ass....kick ass."
—Earnhardt on being relentless.

season. "We just kept racing, trying to win the race. We didn't talk about being careful before the race, either. We just wanted to go out and do a good job. We knew we had to work hard and be competitive in the pits and on the track. We had 500 miles of racing to think about.

"I didn't even see Darrell fall out. They did tell me on the radio that he had gone behind the wall. I said, 'Are you sure?' Then later, under a caution, I said, 'Is that No. 11 car still behind the wall?' They said, 'Yeah, he's even gone home.'

"I never backed off," he added. "I knew we couldn't break our stride. If you pull up on a horse, it wouldn't ride as good. If the car couldn't run the pace I wanted, I would have run its pace. But that wasn't necessary.

"When you go out to kick ass…kick ass."

After the demise of Gant and Shepherd, Neil Bonnett put his Johnson/Budweiser Chevrolet into second place. But he was in the midst of a gamble, attempting to complete the last 69 laps of the race without making a pit stop for gas.

He came up short as his fuel supply ran out with one lap remaining. That dropped him to sixth place, a lap down, and allowed Petty, who made a quick stop on lap 311 for fuel, to move into second place and thereby record his best finish since his triumph in the 1984 Firecracker 400 at Daytona Beach, Fla.

Petty, however, was a lap in arrears and so was Bill Elliott, who finished third in the Coors/Melling Ford. Richmond took fourth, while Buddy Baker put his

Crisco Oldsmobile Delta 88 in fifth place. Both, too, were a lap down.

Rounding out the top 10 were Bonnett, Kyle Petty in the CITGO/7-Eleven Ford; Terry Labonte in the Hagan/Piedmont Airlines Oldsmobile; Joe Ruttman in the Bernstein/Quaker State Buick LaSabre; and Phil Parsons in the Jackson/Skoal Oldsmobile.

Other than Gant and Shepherd, drivers retiring with mechanical problems included Ron Bouchard, Geoff Bodine, Cale Yarborough, Dave Marcis, Sterling Marlin and Mark Martin.

For Earnhardt, the race victory and the championship culminated a season in which he had experienced great success, few failures and a measure of controversy. Accomplishing what he did before the last race of the season removed some pressure, to be sure, but it did not provide an immediate sense of relief.

"Relief?" said Earnhardt. "No, I don't feel relief. I feel excitement. Anytime you win anything you feel excitement."

And that leads to celebration.

"I imagine the team will do some celebrating later," Earnhardt said with a grin.

"We had planned to go to Riverside to test. We won't now. So that means I'll celebrate by going deer hunting until the end of the week."

And then he will go to Riverside, where he will race simply to have fun. ■

It's Earnhardt In The Wild Winston

Earnhardt Wins Amid Controversial Finish

One of Earnhardt's most spectacular victories was so memorable that it created a legendary myth. His victory over Bill Elliott in the 1987 All-Star race featured the infamous "pass in the grass," which really wasn't a pass at all. Earnhardt held the lead late in the race when he darted through the front stretch grass and nearly lost control of his car in an attempt to keep Elliott behind him. Remarkably, he held onto his car and went on to win the race. In the process, he angered Elliott, sparking another longtime rivalry. "The aggressiveness has gotten out of hand," Elliott said. "This is not Saturday night wrestling."

They wanted a shootout in the third annual running of The Winston. They got it. And an argument or two. And some blown tempers. And a fistfight. And a lot more.

In a wham, bam, controversial 10-lap dash finish, Dale Earnhardt spectacularly avoided disaster and withstood the rage of his rivals to record the victory worth $200,000 at the 1.5 mile Charlotte Motor Speedway. In doing so, Earnhardt became the third different winner in the three-year history of the event and spoiled what had been the perfect dominance of Bill Elliott, who humbled the field in the first two segments of the special race by leading 121 of the 125 laps therein.

So, it came as no surprise that Elliott was frustrated after his loss but, beyond that, he was furious with what he felt were Earnhardt's unsportsmanlike, and dangerous, tactics en route to the victory.

The scenario: The first segment of the event, which ran 75 laps, ended with just three men, Elliott in the Coors/Melling Ford Thunderbird, Geoff Bodine in the Hendrick/Levi Garrett Chevrolet Monte Carlo SS, and Kyle Petty in the Wood Brothers/Citgo Ford, sharing the lead. Elliott led 71 of those 75 laps.

Segment Two: It began after a 10-minute delay during which time all 20 teams in the event made NASCAR-legal alterations to their cars. Nearly all did while Elliott took on four tires and patiently awaited the green flag. No other work was done to his car.

The race resumed and, again, Elliott dominated, if that is a strong enough word. He led all 50 laps of the segment and, when it ended, Earnhardt was running second.

Then came the ten-lap trophy dash. Under the new format of The Winston, these ten laps must be run under

After a wild day on and off the track, Earnhardt became the third different winner in the three-year history of The Winston.

green. Cautions do not count. It's what everyone had been waiting for.

Elliott started on the pole, with Bodine second and Petty third – they are the only race leaders, hence they received the top three starting spots. Earnhardt is in fourth. On the start of the first lap, Bodine jumped to a quick start and nudged ahead of Elliott. But, going into the second turn, Bodine's Chevrolet turned sideways after contact with Elliott's Ford. Bodine looped his car and, remarkably, no one made contact.

But, as that happened, Earnhardt, who had moved into third, shot to the inside and found himself all alone in the lead. The complexion of the race changed dramatically. Even so, it marks the first episode that Elliott will later recall as another disreputable Earnhardt driving tactic.

The caution was displayed and Bodine made a pit stop to change tires. Elliott recovered from the mishap suitably enough to run second to Earnhardt and give chase. There's no doubt he has enough strength in his car, but Earnhardt's team has made enough adjustments to his during the two ten-minute stops to ensure that it, too, is stout.

Elliott immediately rode Earnhardt's rear bumper. Just seven laps from the finish, it becomes clear the war is for real. Coming out of the fourth turn, their cars make contact and Earnhardt is sent into the infield grass at the front trioval. In a remarkable display of driving talent, Earnhardt keeps the car on a straight line through a 150-foot plowing job and roars back onto the asphalt, holding his advantage. But, as he later explained, his hackles were up.

One lap later. As the duo raced into the third turn, Elliott came to the outside of Earnhardt. Clearly displeased with what transpired earlier, Earnhardt squeezed Elliott to the wall. He claimed he never made contact. Elliott said otherwise and allowed that it was at this point Earnhardt's maneuver crumpled the left-rear fender onto the tire. The damage was sufficient to cut the tire, resulting in its demise just a lap later.

While the two drivers indulged in this episode, Terry Labonte snaked into the lead in his Johnson/Budweiser Chevrolet. But his advantage did not last long. Earnhardt roared past by the time the field raced into the first turn. He went on to win by 0.74 second. Elliott, after a pit stop to change tires, came home 14th.

But that was far from the end of it. On the final lap, Elliott's Ford limped around the track like a crippled soldier. As Earnhardt raced toward the checkered flag, an obvious winner over Labonte, he closed in on the Coors/Melling Ford. Suddenly, on the backstretch, Elliott's car found life and sped toward the finish line.

Then, on the "cool-down" lap, Elliott's displeasure became obvious. He blocked Earnhardt coming out of the first turn. On the backstretch, he turned toward Earnhardt, on the outside, and forced him to hit the brakes so hard smoke billowed from the tires. He cut his rival off at the entrance to pit road and then, at the entrance to the garage area, he once again turned toward Earnhardt and forced him to move to the outside of pit road.

This was done in the presence of the Wrangler crew, who, ironically, pitted just one space away from Elliott's team. Words were exchanged; fists shook.

It wasn't over. In the garage area, Kyle Petty and Rusty Wallace, driver of the Blue Max/Kodiak Grand Prix 2+2, exchanged blows and were separated by Richard Petty, Kyle's father.

The final rundown showed that behind Earnhardt and Labonte, Tim Richmond finished third in his first race in the Hendrick/Folgers Chevrolet since being felled by double pneumonia in December. Bodine wound up fourth, with Wallace fifth, Kyle Petty sixth, Morgan Shepherd seventh in the Bernstein/Quaker State Buick LaSabre, Bobby Allison eighth in the Stavola/Miller American Buick, Darrell Waltrip ninth in the Hendrick/Tide Chevrolet and Benny Parsons tenth in the Jackson/Copenhagen Oldsmobile Delta 88.

Elliott earned $110,150 for his day's work, $100,000 of which came in leader bonuses through the race's first two segments. He stood to pocket $300,000 with a victory.

His side of the tale: "It really got started (on the final 10 laps) at the start. The pace car didn't get out of the way quickly enough. Geoff got a good start but the pace car was in my way and I couldn't keep up. When we got to the corner, Earnhardt got in front of me and he turned left on me. He hit me. I don't know what happened with Bodine, whether he cut down on me or what, but the next thing I know we are both spinning all of a sudden.

"A lot of things are going on when the green flag drops. I don't know exactly what happened, but it was a situation that never should have happened.

"Then we went into the fourth turn and Earnhardt turned left on me and tried to run me through the grass. I did what I could to keep us both off the grass and wrecking. Then the next thing, well, when a man pulls alongside you and tries to run you into the wall, that's pretty obvious. I had the position. He let me get alongside him and then turned into me. That's when the tire was cut. It crumpled the left fender onto the tire and a couple of laps later it blew. You look at the tape. He hit me several times. The fans saw it. You saw it.

"Yes, when the race was over, I was still ticked off. I admit it. If a man has to run over you to beat you, it's time to stop. I'm sick of it. Everyone knows his style. I am sick and tired of it. If that is what it takes to be the Winston Cup champion, I don't want it.

"The aggressiveness has gotten out of hand. This is not Saturday night wrestling. I've been to Talladega, Daytona and everywhere else and I'm beat up by the same guy.

"Yes, I'm frustrated. My car worked good here. It ran good. I think that was obvious. If you had a car that ran that good only to have it all taken away from you the way it was, how would you feel?

"I think that more than racing, he discredits his sponsor and himself. But I have nothing to say to him. If that is the way he wants to win races, then I hope he wins 1,000 of them. He'll be doing it all on Saturday nights."

With his victory, Earnhardt laid claim to wins in the last four Charlotte events. He swept both the Coca-Cola and the Oakwood Homes 500 in Winston Cup competition last year and won the fall All-Pro 300 Busch Series race. For his career, he has won $709,748 in Winston Cup competition at CMS and $885,673 overall. In the last 12 months, the total is $380,200 for Winston Cup racing, $455,095 overall.

Despite almost coming to post-race blows with Bill Elliott's crew, Team Childress is all smiles in victory lane.

> **"The aggressiveness has gotten out of hand. This is not Saturday night wrestling. I've been to Talladega, Daytona and everywhere else and I'm beat up by the same guy."** —Bill Elliott

His comments after The Winston: "Bodine and Elliott wrecked in the first turn. I guess Bodine chopped down on him and turned him around, but all I know is that I didn't touch anybody. I guess it was reflexes. I checked up and I started to move where I thought they wouldn't be. I decided to go to the bottom of the track and I was by myself. I don't know why they threw the caution flag. No one was stopped.

"Then, as we came into the trioval two laps later, Elliott got under me and clipped me sideways. I almost got the car started the other way before I went into the grass and then I was able to get it right while I was in it. If I hadn't, I might have gone right up into the flagstand right there with Harold Kinder (flagman). I can guarantee you that, if I had turned someone side-ways like that, I would be hanging from the flagpole right now.

"I wasn't upset earlier, but that got me upset.

"On the next lap, he got alongside me on the outside and I took him up the track, but I never touched him. That's when Labonte got by and I knew then I had to race him.

"Bill got frustrated. Look, if I had done what he had through the first two segments of the race only to lose in the last 10 laps, I would be frustrated, too. He waited on me after the checkered flag and then tried to run me into the wall. That was very unsportsmanlike. After that, I tried to stay away from him. I motioned my crew to stay away from his. This was between me and Bill. Not between Ernie (Elliott's brother and crew chief) or anyone else. No one else was on the track.

"I'm not mad at Elliott. I know he was frustrated. If he wants to carry this on, then we will. I will stand flatfooted against him."

Said Cecil Gordon, the former driver who serves as the shop foreman for the Wrangler team owned by Richard Childress: "All you have to do is print what you saw. We've taken the heat from NASCAR at Bristol (Tenn.) and Richmond (Va.) and to have what happened after the race was over, well NASCAR has to do something about it."

Elliott agreed, but in a different way: "I think the only way to stop this is to start fining points. Take them away in cases like this."

NASCAR officials, who stated in the pre-race drivers' meeting that no protests would be allowed since The Winston was a special event that awarded no points, said that they would study videotapes of the final 10 laps and, if needed, make a determination of disciplinary action within a few days.

Elliott won the pole for the event with a track record of 170.827 mph, posted in time trials on May 16. That bettered the one-lap mark of 169.252 mph set by Richmond last October. Richmond was second in qualifying with a lap of 170.23 mph in the Hendrick/Folgers Chevrolet, while Davey Allison was the third man to beat the record with a lap of 169.274 mph in the Ranier/Havoline Ford.

For the record, Earnhardt now has won seven of the 10 events staged this season, although The Winston has no part in the Winston Cup championship and is not listed as an official event as such. He won with an average speed of 153.023 mph. The race had only one official caution flag, thrown when Neil Bonnett and Richard Petty collided in the fourth turn on lap 64. Bonnett, taken to Cabarrus Memorial Hospital for treatment, was released with water on his elbow and right knee. His arm was placed in a sling. ■

Earnhardt Back In Form With AIR Win

Earnhardt Is The Dominator Once Again

Earnhardt's first efforts with new sponsor GM Goodwrench didn't take long to bear fruit, as the defending series champion dusted the field in Atlanta, handily pulling away from rival Rusty Wallace to score his 32nd career Cup win. Following a successful association with sponsor Wrangler, the new black and silver GM paint scheme suited the hard-charging driver perfectly, and set into motion the evolution of Earnhardt into the Man In Black.

They can't say he didn't warn 'em.

Dale Earnhardt, never one to mince words, came right to the point following qualifying for the Motorcraft 500 NASCAR Winston Cup race on March 19.

Taking the No. 2 starting position and eclipsing the old track record in the process, Earnhardt grinned and said, "They better get ready. I'm gonna unload on all of 'em tomorrow."

He did just that. Boy, did he ever.

In the swashbuckling style that has characterized his career, Earnhardt routed the field on the way to victory in the Motorcraft 500. It was the first victory in 1988 for the defending Winston Cup champion and his first since he won the Wrangler Indigo 400 at Richmond (Va.)

Fairgrounds Raceway on Sept. 13, 1987. He thus ended a 10-race losing streak.

It was also the first Winston Cup triumph for Earnhardt wearing the black and silver colors of his new sponsor, GM Goodwrench. With the combination of skill, excellent pit work by his Kirk Shelmerdine-led pit crew and a flawless Childress/GM Goodwrench Chevrolet Monte Carlo SS, Earnhardt led 270 of the race's 328 laps and finished 1.5 seconds ahead of Rusty Wallace in the Blue Max/Kodiak Pontiac Grand Prix SE.

Wallace was that close only because of a late caution. When Bill Elliott's Melling/Coors Ford Thunderbird crashed into the second-turn wall on lap 318, it brought out the day's seventh and final caution period. Cleanup crews moved Elliott's battered car to the infield in time for just three more laps of racing.

While Wallace was poised to make a last-ditch effort, he never mounted an attack; it was something he had been unable to do all day. As he had done throughout the entire event, Earnhardt blasted away from his rivals on the restart and went on to win the 32nd race of his career.

"I said we would be tough because we tested good down here and had a good qualifying run," said the 36-year-old Earnhardt. "I really thought we would win the pole and we missed it by a tick. That was the driver or maybe the tire stagger.

"Once I passed (Geoff) Bodine on the first lap, I felt I had the car to beat all day long. We stayed with our game plan all day. We wanted to put the pressure on everyone else. We came in a couple of times and put four tires on the car during the green and that enabled us to put a couple of cars a lap down. We went out and lapped everybody but Rusty."

Earnhardt's only serious challenge came from Benny Parsons, driver of Junie Donlavey's Bull's Eye Barbecue Sauce Ford. Parsons started eighth, charged through the field and by lap 69 had snatched the lead away from Earnhardt. He held it for one lap, then retook it on lap 87. He held it during the day's fourth caution, created by A.J. Foyt's blown engine because he did not pit.

Earnhardt, however, did. And, when the race resumed on lap 91, he was in 17th place.

Earnhardt's car began to show its power. By lap 96, Earnhardt was fifth. He was fourth on lap 98 and third on lap 101. By lap 105, he had passed Kyle Petty's Wood Brothers/Citgo Ford to take second place.

On lap 114, Earnhardt snatched the lead from Parsons and was in control again. It would stay that way as he led 190 of the remaining 214 laps.

On lap 200, Earnhardt pitted under green and had four tires changed in 22.2 seconds by his crew, three times the Rockingham/Unocal pit crew champions. By lap 213, after the other leaders had pitted for just two tires each, Earnhardt was in front again, tops among the eight cars on the lead lap.

Twenty-five laps later, there were just five cars on the lead lap. Then, Earnhardt did it again. He dashed into the pits on lap 254 and made another four-tire change, this one accomplished in 22.9 seconds. At the time, he held an 11.30-second lead over Parsons.

"We kept getting a larger lead with four fresh tires and we had the cushion we needed to make the stops, so why not use it? Those two stops were the best I had ever seen," Earnhardt said. "We changed four tires in about the same times it takes a lot of teams to change two.

"No, I didn't worry about blistering new tires. We were on Goodyears, and Goodyear has worked hard over the last five days to get us a good tire for here and Darlington (S.C.). They are working as hard as we are to win races."

Parsons moved to the front and held a 22.9-second pad – nearly three-quarters of a lap. Earnhardt moved back into second place by lap 264, but he was still well behind. Parsons, whose pit stops were out of synch with the other leaders, had only to stop for two tires to maintain a still-strong lead.

But disaster struck. Parsons' Ford slowed dramatically in the first turn on lap 206 and it was clear he had run out of gas. He had gone 60 laps, or 90 miles, since his last stop and it was just too much.

"They better get ready. I'm gonna unload on all of 'em tomorrow." — Earnhardt's pre-race prediction.

Earnhardt flew by the competition to record his first Winston Cup victory as "the man in black."

As Parsons limped into the pits for a stop, which would cost him the lead, Earnhardt retook the lead. He never surrendered it, pacing the field for the final 63 circuits.

Meanwhile, Parsons was reduced to making a Sunday drive. His engine suffered a burnt piston and the Ellerbe, N.C., driver who has not won a race since the Motorcraft 500 of 1984 – 76 events ago – came home in 13th place, six laps down.

But, it was the best performance of the year for his team. "I hope the team gets a lift out of this one, because it's only the fourth race we've ever been together," said Parsons. "When my car ran out of gas, it felt like my dog died. But today, we got it all together."

Earnhardt agreed. "Benny ran about as consistent as I did," he said. "He didn't surprise me because he ran good in practice. This is one of his good tracks. So is Darlington (site of the March 27 TranSouth 500)."

When Parsons was forced to leave the track after running out of fuel, Darrell Waltrip moved into second place in his Hendrick Tide Chevrolet. But on lap 270, he was forced to pit and lost a lap to Earnhardt.

That put Kyle Petty in second place, but his pit stop on lap 276 put him a lap down also. That left only Earnhardt and Wallace on the lead lap.

Richard Petty's STP Pontiac dropped a cylinder on lap 297 and that brought out the day's sixth caution period. This allowed Wallace, who was 20.67 seconds behind Earnhardt, to move in behind his old rival on the restart, which came on lap 302.

Wallace couldn't mount a charge and Earnhardt was ahead by 3.2 seconds when Elliott brought out the final caution, which offered Wallace a second chance, one he could not utilize.

"Dale was just too tough," said Wallace. "We definitely had the second-toughest car and I ran my butt off. But Dale was just too tough."

"I really didn't know what would happen and I was concerned there at the end," said Earnhardt. "What if Rusty didn't pit during the caution and we never got back to green? It looked like they were taking a lot of time to get Bill's car off the track. And I could have gotten a set of tires that were too tight or loose and his could have been perfect."

Neither scenario developed, however.

Elliott, a favorite at AIR, started third but was out of contention early. He lost six laps in the pits when a faulty distributor was replaced, beginning on lap 31. Then came his race-closing accident.

Terry Labonte came home in fourth in the Johnson/ Budweiser Chevrolet while Kyle Petty rounded out the top five. Taking sixth place was Bobby Hillin in the Stavola/ Miller High Life Buick Regal; Buddy Baker was seventh in the Red Baron Pizza Oldsmobile Cutlass; Ken Schrader took eighth in the Hendrick/Folgers Chevrolet; Brett Bodine was ninth in the Moore/Crisco Ford and Rick Wilson rounded out the top 10 in the Kodak Oldsmobile.

Earnhardt's victory quelled the talk that the two-time champion was in a slump.

"I'm asked that all the time, 'What's wrong?'" said Earnhardt, who dominated last year's Motorcraft 500 until a broken alternator ruined his victory chances with just 14 laps to go. "We have worked very hard to repeat as champions. But we've had a problem here and a flat tire there, things like that.

"We tried to figure out what was wrong and all it was is that you make your own luck and to do that you just work harder. That's what I think we did and I think we've proven we can dominate again and win races again."

Perhaps he and his team can do more. The victory moved Earnhardt into second place in the Winston Cup point standings with 628 points, just four fewer than leader Neil Bonnett. Bonnett suffered engine problems in his Rahmoc/Valvoline Pontiac and had to coast to a 22nd place finish, 39 laps down.

"Boy it's time to put pressure on Neil now," said Earnhardt, who won with an average speed of 137.588 mph in the three-hour, 37-minute, 42-second race.

"He'd better get going."

After Earnhardt's prediction for the Motorcraft 500, Bonnett might do well to listen. ◼

He warned 'em. Earnhardt predicted a dominating victory and he got it in the Motorcraft 500.

At Last, Daytona Is A Breeze For Earnhardt

Scores First Winston Cup Win At Track With Dominating Form

Five months after a cut tire kept Earnhardt from winning the Daytona 500, the Intimidator scored his first Cup points win at the legendary 2.5-mile track.

At last, Lady Luck embraced Dale Earnhardt at Daytona International Speedway.

Her favor and the undeniable competitiveness of his Richard Childress Chevrolet combined to help give the Kannapolis, N.C., native the victory in the Pepsi 400 and the first NASCAR Winston Cup win of his career on the 2.5-mile speedway.

Although Earnhardt had won 10 times in 56 starts on NASCAR's premier track, not once before had he claimed a Winston Cup victory. He almost had it in February when a cut tire on the last lap forced him to give way to Derrike Cope.

That was undoubtedly one of the most disappointing moments in Earnhardt's career, in which he has now fashioned 44 victories.

Earnhardt dominated again, just as he had in February. This time, however, he avoided misfortune – not once, but twice.

"It's not the Daytona 500, but it's one I've never won," said Earnhardt, who had his 13th career start in the Pepsi 400. "Daytona is one of my favorite places. This is the same car we ran at Daytona earlier this year and at Talladega (Ala.).

"We felt if we got it close, we would be all right."

Earnhardt started third but snatched the lead away from pole winner Greg Sacks as the field entered the first and second turns on the first lap. It was good that he did because, just as the lap was completed, one of the most spectacular wrecks in recent years was triggered.

Earnhardt goes high on the competition. Most of the day, he just went by them.

Sacks was caught between the cars of Richard Petty, on the inside, and Cope, on the outside, as the three jockeyed for position behind Earnhardt. A little jostling was all it took. Cope and Sacks made contact on the frontstretch and Sacks' Chevrolet clipped the right-rear of Petty's Pontiac, which was turned sideways.

With the track effectively blocked, the field of cars turned into a spinning, smoking mass. By the time the melee had ended, 23 cars had become involved in one way or another.

Many of the drivers figured to challenge for the victory – Petty, Sacks, Ernie Irvan, Morgan Shepherd, Mark Martin, Cope and others – were either eliminated from the race or so severely crippled they could only limp home after repairs.

"I hate to see things like that happen," said Earnhardt. "I'm a competitive driver and the others are competitive drivers. You don't want things like wrecks and injury to happen.

"I wish all of them had stayed in the race. I think our Chevrolet was strong enough to handle them."

There was plenty of evidence. Earnhardt led the first 31 laps, giving way to Jimmy Spencer during the second

caution period, brought out after the right-rear tire in Elliott's Ford gave out and forced him to clip the second-turn wall.

Earnhardt retook the lead by lap 35 and held it for 27 circuits. He then made an unscheduled pit stop on lap 62 for right-side tires.

"The car had picked up a push," Earnhardt explained. "I had seen what happened to Bill when he crashed after having a flat right-rear tire. I told Richard on the radio I didn't want to take any chances and that I wanted to pit to get tires. I didn't want a right-front going flat.

"That put us out of sync with the others, as far as pit stops were concerned, but then we got another caution and that put us back."

Before that, however, Earnhardt had reassumed the lead after his rivals made their scheduled pit stops under the green flag. On lap 80, Rob Moroso pitted to allow Earnhardt's Chevrolet to once again take the point. It had a whopping 13.1-second margin over Harry Gant's Oldsmobile.

The third caution came on lap 91 when Martin spun his Ford out of the second turn. Now back in sync, as far as pit stops were concerned, Earnhardt remained in front when green-flag racing resumed on lap 96.

But where he once held sway with conviction, he now had to contend with the surprisingly strong Bobby Hillin. Although Earnhardt kept Hillin's Buick at bay easily for several laps, by lap 128 of the 160-lap race, Hillin had taken advantage of Earnhardt's handling problems to close on his rear bumper and threaten to pass.

"The car was a little tight in the corners and that's why Hillin could catch up," Earnhardt explained. "It would push more as the gas was used up.

"One time, Bobby tried to race me but I slowed both of us up. So I waved to him to stay in line and that sped us up."

There was one final scheduled pit stop to be made and Earnhardt made his on lap 134.

"We didn't change any tires," he said. "We knocked the spoiler down a bit, took out a round of wedge and the car was perfect after that."

Then Hillin, the new leader, pitted on lap 139. It would be his downfall.

He charged into the pits too hard and looped his car at his pit area, nearly taking out front-tire changer Tim Petty in the process. His crew refilled his gas tank and pushed him away, the stop having taken 24 seconds and dropping him well back in the lead pack.

"If he would have made a clean pit stop, he would have been the one I was racing at the end," Earnhardt said.

Gant, Ken Schrader, Kulwicki and Moroso each led the race – giving way for pit stops – until Earnhardt took over on lap 144 when Moroso pitted. He was in front of Kulwicki by 7.5 seconds.

By lap 150, Earnhardt had expanded that lead to 10.3 seconds, but he was denied a stroll to the finish. On

lap 154, J.D. McDuffie, driving his Pontiac, which had started with Dave Marcis behind the wheel, spun in the first turn – in front of Earnhardt.

"I saw it happen and it was very close," said Earnhardt, who earned $72,850 for his victory. "I locked the car down and dodged the right way.

"I just did the best I could under the circumstances and I got out of the way."

Earnhardt's luck was holding out. But the fourth and final caution period allowed Kulwicki, making his best run of the season, to close on Earnhardt's bumper at the restart, which came on lap 158. There were three laps left.

Earnhardt got a tremendous jump as the green flag fell. Kulwicki could not challenge. All that remained for Earnhardt was to hope that the same, last-lap misfortune, which cost him the Daytona 500 victory, would not happen again.

"Alan was laying off me pretty good as we got into the third turn," said Earnhardt. "So I slowed down to back up to him. Then, when we got to the grass at the fourth turn, where we're supposed to start, I did.

"We've been working on our engines to help us get off the corners and that's helped us with restarts. That's how I got by Sacks and Elliott at the start of the race, too.

"On the last lap, I drove in the middle groove. I didn't want to drive on the edges and take the chance of getting into some debris. I wanted to run it smooth. I had gotten away from Alan and just wanted to get back to the line.

"That's when I would win the race and I didn't think about winning until I got there."

The three-time Winston Cup champion got there 1.47 seconds ahead of Kulwicki, with Schrader

"It's not the Daytona 500, but it's one I've never won." — Earnhardt

third, Terry Labonte fourth and Sterling Marlin fifth. Rounding out the top 10 were Hillin, Gant, Dale Jarrett, Moroso and Kyle Petty.

Earnhardt's finish catapulted him back into second place in the Winston Cup point standings. Martin, despite his problems, retains the lead with 2,221 points but Earnhardt is just 63 points behind with 2,158. The big loser was Shepherd. Hobbled by the race-opening crash, he finished 34th and fell from second to fifth in the standings after losing 69 points.

Not only did the Pepsi 400 win change Earnhardt's fortunes at Daytona, it also enhanced his performance record of late. It was his second straight win and his fifth of the season, coming after a four-race dry spell that dropped him from No. 1 in the point standings.

Prior to Michigan, mechanical problems and accidents had sent Earnhardt spiraling to finishes of 30th, 31st, and 34th in the three consecutive events before he struggled to a 13th-place at Pocono, Pa., on June 17, one week before Michigan.

"You go through your spells of bad luck," said Earnhardt, who averaged 160.894 mph in his victory. You just have to work hard and things will come back to you.

"Now we've won the Pepsi 400 and who knows? It's a lot different than the Daytona 500. There are 100 more miles in that race. We'll just have to race here in 1991 and see what happens.

"We've been getting right back to where we need to be. We want to be as competitive as we can. We want to keep the consistency we've found in the last two races for the rest of the season." ∎

It's good work, if you can get it.

Earnhardt: Back In Form With Victory in Coca-Cola 600

Earnhardt Makes It All Happen

A fast green-flag pit stop late in the race helped Earnhardt to this victory. That's not what made it a big one. The victory was his first one in the 600-miler in six years. That's important but not huge. The Charlotte win was his first in 14 races. That's not necessarily what made it a big one, either. The fact that Ford drivers had won the 13 races since his last win? That's what made it a big deal. Synonymous with Chevrolet, Earnhardt broke that Ford streak.

It took a while, but Dale Earnhardt and General Motors have found their way back into victory lane.

Earnhardt, the defending NASCAR Winston Cup champion, held off Ernie Irvan in a nail-biter of a finish to win the Coca-Cola 600 and thus record his first victory of the season and allow GM to snap Ford's 13-race victory streak.

For the 41-year-old Earnhardt, the victory was his first since he won in North Wilkesboro, N.C., in October of 1991, 13 races ago. Ironically, Ford's streak began a week later when Geoff Bodine took the checkered flag in the Mello Yello 500 at CMS.

But upon the return visit to the 1.5-mile Charlotte track, it was not to be Ford's day as the race boiled down to a scrap among a trio of GM cars – and ultimately hinged on the outcome of the final pit stops.

When the checkered flag fell, Earnhardt had successfully kept Irvan at bay by 0.39 second, or about three car lengths. For the native of Kannapolis, N.C., it was his 53rd career victory – and certainly one of his most satisfying, since he became the man who put GM back in the spotlight.

"It feels great," said Earnhardt of the win, which earned him $125,100. "It feels great to be the one to stop Ford's streak and it feels especially good to win in my 400th career start.

"I said before the race it was time for something big to happen. That's why I picked Richard Petty to win the race. But he didn't and I did. And, to me, that's big – believe me."

Earnhardt was in position to win as the laps wound down. But he was in an even better position to finish third, behind Kyle Petty in the Sabco Pontiac and Irvan, driver of the Morgan-McClure Chevy. Petty, in fact, led

the most laps in the race (141) and was in front of Irvan when the two pitted for the final time on lap 346 of the 400-lap race.

Petty's stop took 19.72 seconds for four new tires while Irvan spent 21.19 seconds on pit road for the same service. By leaving the track, they elevated Earnhardt –

Earnhardt takes the lead on defending Coca-Cola 600 winner Davey Allison, who finished fourth.

who had been a distant third – into the lead for the first time in the race.

Earnhardt took over on lap 347. On lap 348, he darted into the pits for his final stop. It would be a real test for his pit crew, four-time winners of the world championship pit crew competition.

Earnhardt came down pit road as quickly as he could within NASCAR rules, which dictate a specific, slow entrance. His crew then performed a four-tire change in 19.40 seconds, 0.32 second quicker than Petty's team. Earnhardt left the pits, sped around the return lane low around turns one and two and came back onto the track still in first place.

That made all the difference.

"That pit stop was the key," said Earnhardt. "The guys did a great job and I probably fudged as much as I could coming down pit road. When we tested the tachometer coming down pit road on the pace lap (required by NASCAR), mine read 4,000 rpms in second gear. When I came down pit road the last time, I kept it at 4,050 rpms.

"Then I got out of the pits as quick as I could and came through the lane there in one and two pretty quick, too."

Although Earnhardt's stop befuddled a few observers and fellow competitors – particularly Petty, who felt there was no way his rival could emerge in first place by one second – the fact remained Earnhardt had gained the advantage.

"By being in front, it meant the others behind me would have to run their tires harder to catch up while I could work on saving mine," he said. "That was the key to beating Ernie because, even though he was strong, I had the edge. I couldn't get him when he was in front of me."

Over the last 53 laps, Irvan gave a strong effort. At times, Earnhardt would pull out to a three- or four-car length advantage. But then, Irvan would make up the distance, usually in turn three, and close on his opponent's rear bumper.

But he never had the chance to pass.

"I ran my line, " said Earnhardt. "In turns three and four, the car would push a little in the middle and I had to be careful because then the car would push out and I didn't want Ernie to get under me.

"I was extra cautious and I wanted him to make a move on me or take another line. I was a bit surprised at Ernie there, but I have to admit he raced me clean and hard and he's really coming around as a race driver."

Irvan made an attempt to take the high route on the last lap, but it was to no avail.

"He did try the outside, but his car wouldn't hold," Earnhardt said.

Most of the race belonged to Petty, who was bidding to win his first race of the season as well. He had led 102 of 104 laps from circuits 243-346 before the final pit stops began. But the handling characteristics of his Pontiac changed at the finish and he couldn't keep up. He finished third, about three seconds in arrears.

Meanwhile, Davey Allison, driver of the Robert Yates Racing Ford and defending winner of the Coca-Cola 600 who was bidding to win his fourth race of the season and a $1 million bonus in the Winston Million program, fell short. He finished fourth after leading 33 laps. He can still claim the bonus with a victory in the Mountain Dew Southern 500 at Darlington (S.C.) Raceway on September 6.

The first half of the race was characterized by "stop-and-go" racing due to a rash of caution periods. There were 10 by the time the event was 204 laps old, eight of which fell between laps 101 and 185. Nearly all were caused by crashes, which Earnhardt avoided.

"Boy, there were some close calls," he said. "One time I went down pit road at full speed to avoid one and another time I went through the grass on the frontstretch. I was lucky not to get caught up in any of them and wreck the car or knock the front end out or anything, but it was close."

Earnhardt wasn't a factor for most of the race. That was due to the fact his car wasn't handling properly. But, all things considered, he was lucky to have the car at all. He utilized the one that was wrecked on the last

Earnhardt and GM snap Ford's 13-race winning streak.

> # "Charlotte had been a great track for me; a lot of great things have happened to me [here]." —Earnhardt

lap of The Winston on May 16 in an altercation with Petty.

Hasty repairs were made to restore the car for the Coca-Cola 600. Among the repairs were replacement of the rear frame, rear quarter panel, trunk deck, left front fender, A-frame. The chassis was taken out and a new engine put in.

"The repairs should have taken over a week but the guys worked all day Sunday and Monday and the body guys worked overnight," said Earnhardt. "The car was primed and painted in one night. Everything worked out and we had the car here Wednesday (May 20).

"But it was very loose at the start. We took the pan out from the front end but then that's when it picked up the little push later in the race. It was really good through turns one and two but the push came between three and four. We were sacrificing there but we held 'em off."

Harry Gant, in the Leo Jackson Oldsmobile, followed Allison in fifth place while Terry Labonte took sixth in the Hagan Racing Oldsmobile. Seventh place went to Alan Kulwicki in the Kulwicki Racing Ford while Ted Musgrave posted an eighth-place finish in the RaDiUs Racing Chevrolet, Ricky Rudd was ninth, in the Hendrick Motorsports Chevrolet, and Dick Trickle, in the Stavola Brothers Ford, was 10th.

The rash of accidents proved fatal to Richard Petty, driver of the Petty Enterprises Pontiac, who was involved in three incidents. Early in the race, Petty ran as high as eighth place before being eliminated and relegated to a 41st-place finish.

Engine failure or accidents claimed or hampered Mark Martin, Hut Stricklin, Geoff Bodine, Morgan Shepherd, Jimmy Spencer, Ken Schrader, Michael Waltrip, Sterling Marlin, Brett Bodine and Bobby Hamilton. Earnhardt's victory was his first in the Coca-Cola 600 since 1986. Until this race, his best finish had been a pair of thirds at Talladega, Ala., and Atlanta.

"Charlotte had been a great track for me; a lot of great things have happened to me," said Earnhardt, who now has four career victories at the track. "But a lot bad has happened to me, too. Even though I've won a couple of The Winstons since 1986, I hadn't won the 600 or the 500 in the fall. It was good for me and the team to get back into victory lane."

Earnhardt's victory also propelled him into fifth place in the Winston Cup championship point standings, 144 points behind leader Allison with 19 races remaining in the season.

"We still feel good about the championship," Earnhardt said. "We look at the points situation at every race. We want to run good and consistent and be there at the end of each race and, today, we were first at the finish.

"But the main goal is to keep the car consistent because that is what is going to win the championship."

Earnhardt didn't hesitate to say he felt pleased to be the man to end Ford's streak.

"I feel great to be the one to stop it," he said. "I'm just sorry it took so long.

"But I don't like to run second to anyone. When we're not in victory lane and Fords are, it's not good. Hey, when I was following Kyle and Ernie, I wasn't happy to see them in front of me.

"But the pressure is on the corporate side. It's not on me or the team. This is definitely a turnaround for us and all the GM teams."

Perhaps those words will prove prophetic, indeed. ∎

Penalties Don't Stop Earnhardt

Veteran Is First To Reach $17 Million In Career Winnings

When NASCAR and Charlotte Motor Speedway decided to end its longest race under the lights, it was made for an Earnhardt-like moment. Earnhardt won the Coca-Cola 600 for the third time, but not without creating some fireworks. He rallied from a lap down twice and overcame a penalty for rough driving to win the race. At one point, NASCAR black-flagged him for intentionally spinning Greg Sacks to bring out a caution flag. "I didn't hit him, per se, hit him. But I might have been again' him," Earnhardt said with a familiar grin.

Dale Earnhardt shook off two penalties and came from a lap down on two occasions to win his second straight Coca-Cola 600 and the third of his NASCAR Winston Cup career.

With the victory, Earnhardt became the first driver to win the circuit's longest race at night when he celebrated by taking a Polish victory lap around the 1.5-mile speedway in honor of the late Alan Kulwicki.

"With this being Charlotte and being so close to Alan's shop and CMS paying tribute to Alan before the race, it seemed only fitting that we do that and the team was really behind it," Earnhardt said, who was the top lap-leader, setting the pace four times for 152 laps in the 400-lap event.

"The team was really behind it, and it felt good to do it. I had a lot of respect for Alan and he was a good champion."

A happy Earnhardt said he "drove hard all day and half the night" to claim the win that made him the first driver to earn consecutive Coca-Cola 600 victories since Darrell Waltrip in 1988-89. And Earnhardt did it with an event record of 145.504 mph. The old record was 145.327 mph set May 25, 1975, by Richard Petty in a Dodge.

"I drove hard all day and it seemed like I was behind after I was ahead," Earnhardt said.

The Kannapolis, N.C., native now has 55 Winston Cup career wins, giving him sole possession of sixth on the series' all-time victory list. Prior to the event, he shared the position with Lee Petty at 54.

With his third win this year in a Winston Cup points race, Earnhardt increased his lead in the quest for his sixth title to 129 points over Rusty Wallace. When they entered the event, Earnhardt possessed a 20-point advantage over Wallace.

With this 29th-place finish, Wallace also lost ground to the third-place Dale Jarrett. With his best finish ever in the Coca-Cola 600, Jarrett jumped from sixth to third in the Winston Cup points and found himself just 79 points behind Wallace.

Jarrett, driving a Chevrolet, finished third behind rookie Jeff Gordon. Ken Schrader and Ernie Irvan placed fourth and fifth respectively, both in Chevrolets.

There were 29 lead changes among 10 drivers in the race that took 4 hours 7 minutes and 25 seconds to complete. It was slowed by seven caution flags for 32 laps before an estimated crowd of 162,000.

"The car got better and better as the night got cooler," Earnhardt said. "The car, at the end of the race, was running more like last Saturday night (when Earnhardt won The Winston).

"Andy (Petree, crew chief), (Richard) Childress (car owner) and I ran the same setup that we did last Saturday night. We suffered some at the start.

"We changed a pound of air pressure here and there. We did that for the temperature of the track. Not the chassis, but for the grip."

When the race began at 4:30 p.m., the track's temperature was 120 degrees. At the halfway mark, after 200 laps, it had dropped to 82 degrees, and when the race ended, it was 77 degrees.

Earnhardt also said a chassis adjustment was made with "one turn of wedge."

Earnhardt, 42, won a Coca-Cola 600 record $156,650, thus giving him $905,245 for the season. For his career, Earnhardt became the first driver in motorsports history to reach the $17 million mark with $17,000,027. And in three races during the last week at CMS, Earnhardt collected $380,545. That's $222,500 in The Winston, $1,395 in the Champion Spark Plug 300 Busch Series race, and the rest in the Coca-Cola 600.

For Earnhardt, this year's win in the 600-mile race was probably one of his more difficult ones as he had to overcome two penalties and come from one lap down

on two separate occasions. Also, during his first pit stop, one of his tire carriers slipped and was tagged by Gordon's Chevrolet, which was pitting directly behind Earnhardt.

"It's really satisfying to win after getting penalized," Earnhardt said. "To get a lap penalty, as competitive as everybody is, you would think you might have a bad time making it up. To make it up early as easy as we did, we caught a caution and we were lucky there. Then we got back to the lead pretty good. That says something for the race car and the team."

NASCAR assessed Earnhardt a 15-second penalty on lap 221 for entering pit road too fast.

"Was I going too fast on pit road?" Earnhardt asked the media in his post-race interview. "I don't know how fast I was going on pit road but the 28 (Davey Allison) was catching me."

During that green-flag pit stop, Earnhardt lost a lap and when Wallace spun off turn two and his Pontiac hit the inside wall, that left only Jarrett and Bobby Labonte

Earnhardt held off charging rookie Jeff Gordon to win the Coca-Cola 600 and become the first driver to top $17 million in career earnings.

on the lead lap when the fifth-caution flag appeared. It also allowed Jarrett and Labonte to pit under yellow.

Earnhardt passed the two leaders on the restart, thus putting him on the tail end of the lead lap. With 100 laps remaining, Earnhardt had made his way into second but he was a half lap behind leader Jarrett.

Then, on lap 327, Greg Sacks' Ford spun off turn four and NASCAR ruled, after watching a video replay and talking with Sacks' crew chief Dave Fuge, that Earnhardt would be penalized one lap for rough driving.

"We looked at the replays of the incident five or six times and there was absolutely no question in our minds of what happened in turn four and why it happened." NASCAR spokesman Chip Williams said in a prepared statement distributed to the media.

"We also checked with the driver of the 68 car (Sacks) and he confirmed what we had seen.

"The incident was uncalled for. We instituted the penalty and that made up for any advantage the 3 car might have gained."

After the race, Sacks statement didn't match what NASCAR said he told the sanctioning body earlier. Sacks said, "If Dale touched me, it was just because we were racing hard. He took the air off my car and I got loose. If Dale touched me, it didn't matter."

"I didn't hit him, per se, hit him," Earnhardt said. "I caught a lap penalty for it, so undoubtedly, they (NASCAR) think I hit him. He says I hit him. We got the lap back and won the race, so it's neither here nor there, is it?

"I still won't say I hit him. If we rubbed or the bumpers touched a bit, it wasn't like I just went up there and knocked the crap out of him and turned him over or around or whatever. I don't think I nudged him. I still don't think I hit him."

Since Earnhardt didn't believe he hit Sacks, he was surprised when NASCAR penalized him. He said he came in for a routine pit stop and when he prepared to leave, the NASCAR official assigned to his pit stopped him. Earnhardt thought he was being held on pit road for speeding again.

Earnhardt was able to keep Gordon in his rearview mirror most of the day.

> ## "I'm glad Gordon didn't catch me, He is a tough little driver and he is going to be hard to handle."
> ## —Earnhardt on rookie driver Jeff Gordon

"Richard asked him and he said, 'No, they penalized you a lap for rough driving.' I didn't hit him. All I was thinking about was getting back on the track and trying to make my lap up." Earnhardt said.

On the restart, Earnhardt and Jimmy Spencer immediately passed leader Labonte to get back on the tail end of the lead lap. That maneuver put Earnhardt seventh and Spencer eighth. When Wallace hit the third-turn wall on lap 350, that resulted in the seventh and final caution flag and enabled Earnhardt, Spencer, and Gordon, who lost a lap on a stop-and-go penalty for jumping the previous restart, to come around the track and catch up to the rest of the field. Irvan was the only driver on the lead lap who didn't pit under the final caution, so when the race restarted, he was leading. Mark Martin was second, Schrader was third, Labonte fourth, Jarrett fifth, Gordon sixth, Spencer seventh, Earnhardt eighth, and Bill Elliott ninth.

Martin's Ford blew its engine on lap 355 when the race restarted and Earnhardt quickly clicked off the cars in front of him. On lap 362, Earnhardt went under Irvan for the lead as they raced through turn two and Schrader went with him to take over second. Schrader remained on Earnhardt's bumper for a few laps but then Earnhardt began pulling away. With 11 laps remaining, he held a 2.52-second advantage over Schrader.

With five laps to go, Gordon had taken over second and he trailed Earnhardt by 3.52 seconds.

"I'm glad Gordon didn't catch me," said Earnhardt, who finished 4.1 seconds ahead of Gordon. "He is a tough little driver and he is going to be hard to handle."

Earnhardt qualified 14th for the event and had moved to seventh by lap 20. He was never out of the top 10 the rest of the day, even on the two occasions when he was a lap down.

Earnhardt took the lead for the first time on a daring move on lap 98. Entering turn three, Martin was the leader, but Earnhardt chose the outside while Irvan moved to the inside. With Martin in the center, instead of making it three abreast through turn four, Martin backed off and Earnhardt swept into the lead with Irvan on his bumper.

Earnhardt held the No. 1 spot for the next 38 laps until Joe Ruttman's Ford spun off turn two, causing the third caution flag. Earnhardt pitted, turning the lead over to rookie Rich Bickle who held it for one lap before returning it to Earnhardt when he pitted.

For the next 11 laps, Earnhardt was the person on the point, but then Irvan decided he wanted the position and he grabbed the lead as they entered turn one.

Earnhardt led two other occasions before the event ended. One was for 64 laps – 157-220 and the other was the final 39 laps – 362-400.

With his success this season, Earnhardt said his team's confidence is high.

"You think Andy came in and it made a big difference, well it did," said Earnhardt, who noted Neil Bonnett would test his car this week at Michigan International Speedway.

"But the team had a big rethinking last October, November when Kirk (Shelmerdine, former crew chief) announced he was leaving. So, even before Andy came on board we had a big rethinking. We started working hard at reorganizing at that point. Andy added to that part of the team. And it shows they are getting it done." ■

Dale Earnhardt and Team Memorialize Allison After Pocono Victory

Earnhardt's fifth win of the season came at Pocono, less than a week after the death of fellow driver and friend Davey Allison. Series champion Alan Kulwicki had been killed in an airplane crash earlier in the year. It was Earnhardt's second, and final, win at the oddly-shaped 2.5-mile track, and he paid tribute to the two rivals in prayer at the finish line and with Kulwicki's signature Polish victory lap afterwards.

Dale Earnhardt stopped at the Pocono finish line to remember a friend, then took off on the most appropriate victory lap ever turned. No champion could have done it better.

Earnhardt had just won his fifth race of the season - taking the Miller Genuine Draft 500 – and he further increased his Winston Cup point lead. It mattered little, though, following the death of Davey Allison earlier in the week, and the death of Alan Kulwicki earlier in the season.

So Earnhardt stopped his Chevrolet at the start/finish line and joined his kneeling teammates for a prayer, an emotional end to yet another tragic time for both racing and the Allison family.

Following the prayer, Earnhardt took off on one of Kulwicki's patented Polish victory laps, all while holding a No. 28 flag out his window in honor of Allison.

"I think it all came to heart right there," Earnhardt said of the prayer, led by David Smith, the jackman on the RCR Enterprises team.

"We came in and said a prayer for Davey and Liz and the kids, then took a victory lap in remembrance of Davey and Alan. It's been a tough year, losing two friends.

"I wish I could bring 'em back. We are going to miss 'em."

That moment ended a somber week for the Winston Cup circuit. Allison's death on July 13 marked the second tragedy in four months, and left most emotionally spent after the Pocono race.

"It's really a dark year for racing," Earnhardt's crew chief, Andy Petree, said. "We are really going to miss those guys, Davey and Alan. We're happy, but we've got sadness in our hearts."

That sadness was universal at Pocono. In honor of Davey Allison, all the teams carried a No. 28 on their cars and uniforms. Also, shortly before the race, a lone trumpeter played "Taps" while the flag was lowered to half staff and a crowd of about 100,000 remembered Allison.

"I'd have been glad to run second to him today to have him back," Earnhardt said. "Davey was a heck of a good friend. We didn't hang out all the time, but I hunted and fished with him over the years.

"It's pretty emotional, and tough to describe. There's nothing anybody can say or do – just honor and remember him the best way we can."

Earnhardt did that by winning his second race of the month, leading seven times for 71 laps and holding off Rusty Wallace for the final 17.

A Fitting Tribute. Earnhardt heads out for one of Alan Kulwicki's Polish victory laps while also honoring Davey Allison.

Earnhardt celebrates for the fans after a tough week in the motorsports' family.

The victory also regained some of the points Earnhardt lost after a dismal New Hampshire debut, giving him a 209-point lead over Dale Jarrett (2,612-2,403). Wallace still sits third, 260 back with 2,352.

Ironically, losing 95 points to Wallace the week before primed Earnhardt for Pocono.

"I race better under pressure," he said. "I'm not good at stroking or just being consistent or anything. To have Rusty back in form the last two races and to be a contender is pretty neat."

Neat, when Earnhardt's beating him, that is.

Earnhardt hovered around the lead most of the day. He charged from his 11th-place starting spot to the front by lap 13, and he never fell out of the top five except for green-flag pit stop sequences.

Earnhardt took the lead for good on lap 183 of the 200-lap event, driving by Wallace out of turn one and holding the line into the second turn of the flat, triangular track. He held off Wallace from there, which included a restart on lap 190 after a spin by Jimmy Horton brought out the eighth and final caution.

Wallace chased Earnhardt late, but he never got close enough to challenge for the lead.

"I couldn't catch him, and he couldn't pull away," Wallace said. "We stayed three car lengths apart for 30 laps."

That separation helped the two pull away from a pack that battled hard for the third spot. Bill Elliot led that group, ahead

> # "I'd have been glad to run second to him today to have him back. Davey was a heck of a good friend." —Earnhardt

of Morgan Shepherd, Brett Bodine and pole winner Ken Schrader.

Those four diced throughout the closing laps. Elliot diced the best and, in the process, notched his first top-five finish of an otherwise frustrating season.

"I could see the leaders from there," Elliott said. "Well, at least we could see an improvement.

"It just looked like Rusty and Dale out-powered me. Traffic hurt, but I really think Dale was playing with Rusty. Rusty and I ran together earlier in the day, but Dale could just go on."

Earnhardt said he neither toyed with Wallace nor relaxed much during the race. He did say he raced hard, all the while biding his time for a late sprint.

"I wanted to save my tires there at the end, but those guys behind me started racing hard and we had to go," he said, "I was just going to bide my time. I raced hard all day long and stayed up front most of the day."

Biding his time may have helped Kyle Petty. Petty, who dominated the Pocono race in June, once again drove to the front. He even led twice for 26 laps, and raced Earnhardt and Jarrett hard for the lead several times during the middle stages of the race.

Trying to race out of the pits, though, cost Petty.

After pitting on lap 129 – and while running second to Jarrett, who also pitted on 129 – Petty tore out of his pits in pursuit of Jarrett. Unfortunately for the Sabco Racing team, he tore out the clutch in his Pontiac at the same time.

"We could race with Earnhardt and those guys up front," Petty said. "It was driver error. I just tore the clutch up leaving the pits…I don't know if I could have beaten Earnhardt or not."

Jarrett and Bodine appeared strong enough at times to beat Earnhardt. Jarrett led four times for 48 laps, Bodine once for 14. And both led during the race's second half.

Bodine's laps at the point came as late as 163-176, after he and Wallace didn't pit during the caution that was triggered by Geoff Bodine's spin down the frontstretch. But another caution, this one for oil on the track on 176 brought all the leaders to the pits.

This time, Bodine exited third, behind Wallace and Earnhardt. Four laps after going green on 180, Bodine sat sixth, his chances for an upset victory pushed aside, much like he was in the third turn.

"We had a shot at winning it," said Bodine, who still recorded his first top-five finish since September and only his second since 1990. "But, we got shuffled out of the deal there in three."

After the victory and his tribute to Allison, Earnhardt began looking toward the DieHard 500 at Talladega, Ala.

The race will be bittersweet for Earnhardt – and everyone in racing. Longtime friend Neil Bonnett is set to return to racing in Earnhardt's backup car after three years off because of a head injury.

But overshadowing the week, will be the return to Allison's home track, also the sight of his fatal helicopter crash.

"It's going to be tough next week," Earnhardt said. "The 28 car will probably be back, and seeing it without Davey will be tough.

"Some of the family will probably be there. You can't help but respect the Allisons. It's sad to see a family go through so much, but I think Bobby will bounce back.

"…This is tough for everybody. Anybody involved in racing knows how these teams feel today." ■

 Earnhardt By A Nose Over Irvan Race Punctuated By Two Terrifying Crashes

Earnhardt won this wild affair by 6" over Ernie Irvan. Already an emotional weekend just two weeks after Davey Allison was killed in a helicopter crash at the track, the race included two scary incidents with cars literally flying. Stanley Smith was flown from the track in critical condition after an accident that included Jimmy Horton's car rolling over the concrete retaining wall and landing on its wheels outside the track in an area where there were no grandstands. Neil Bonnett later got airborne in the trioval and tore apart the catch fence, and the race was stopped for more than an hour for repairs to the fence.

After more than an hour delay to repair a damaged catch fence, Dale Earnhardt edged Ernie Irvan by inches to claim his fifth DieHard 500 in a high-speed chess game that had two horrifying crashes in which one driver was critically injured.

Stanley Smith, 43, was flown by helicopter from the 2.66-mile track to Carraway Methodist Medical Center in Birmingham, Ala., after receiving emergency treatment at his race car on the turn two apron.

Also involved in the accident were Kenny Wallace, Rick Mast, Ritchie Petty and Jimmy Horton, whose Chevrolet became airborne in turn one and rolled over the concrete retaining wall. It came to rest on its wheels, outside the track.

It was the first time a car has landed outside the track in an accident since last year at Watkins Glen (N.Y.) International when Greg Sacks' car rolled outside the road course. It was the first time a driver's car has flown over a retaining wall at an oval since June 1979, when Blackie Wangerin sailed out of Michigan International Speedway.

Horton, who walked away from his battered car, said he was "bruised up a little bit." He said he remembered seeing Wallace get sideways, tried to avoid him and then someone hit his Chevrolet in the right rear quarter panel. That's when his car sailed over the wall.

Petty said he believed his Ford ran into Smith's Chevrolet. Petty said when he attempted to move up the track, Smith's car shot up the speedway in front of him.

The other terrible crash occurred on lap 132 when Neil Bonnett's Chevrolet became airborne in the trioval, rolled over and then slammed into the catch fence on the frontstretch. He was thrown back on the grassy apron and stopped right side up.

While Bonnett's Chevrolet was ripping away about 25 feet of catch fence, Ted Musgrave's Ford slammed backwards into the outside wall and the car caught fire as it slid beneath the flagstand.

The race was stopped for 1 hour, 10 minutes and 8 seconds while the fence was repaired. No spectators were injured in the incident.

When the race returned to green flag conditions on lap 140, Earnhardt was third behind Irvan and Ricky Rudd, respectively, and there were 25 cars on the lead lap. For the rest of the way, the leaders were engaged in a high-speed chess game that saw Rudd, Ken Schrader and Jeff Gordon, all key players through most of the event, fall by the wayside with engine problems.

With about 40 laps remaining, rookie Bobby Labonte's Ford latched onto Kyle Petty's Pontiac's rear bumper and for at least three laps, they raced side by side with Irvan and Rudd, who was on Irvan's Chevrolet's rear bumper. Irvan was credited with leading laps 131-146, while Petty set the pace for laps 147-155.

Earnhardt refined his focus before he took to the track and edged Ernie Irvan by inches.

Taylor knows whose dad is No. 1.

On lap 154, pole position winner Bill Elliott, who had run among the leaders throughout the day, got squeezed into the backstretch wall and the toe-in on his Ford was knocked out, causing him to fall out of the lead draft.

Irvan regained the lead from Petty on lap 156 and held the point in the 13-car lead draft for the next eight laps.

Then, on lap 164, Petty moved high to snatch the lead from Irvan. With 20 laps remaining, Petty was still leading, Earnhardt was second, Irvan third, Labonte fourth and Bobby Hillin fifth. Five laps later, the lead draft contained only eight cars with Dale Jarrett trailing Hillin. Then came Mark Martin and Brett Bodine.

On lap 176, Jarrett moved to the outside of Labonte and Martin followed Jarrett. With 12 laps remaining, Martin was notified via his radio that Jarrett wanted to go with him when he pulled out to pass.

Petty still had the lead with five laps remaining, but then Earnhardt made his move. On lap 185, Earnhardt

dropped to the inside of Petty as they raced into turn three and Irvan followed Earnhardt. Jarrett followed and they shuffled Petty back to fourth with Martin fifth and Labonte sixth.

Earnhardt, 42, led the final four laps, but it was no easy task for the North Carolina driver who now has 59 career Winston Cup wins. On lap 187, Earnhardt moved ahead by about five car lengths when the cars behind him began racing side by side. But that quickly changed on the white-flag lap as Earnhardt remained high and Irvan moved to the inside.

"I don't know how we all mixed up and got to where we were, but we (Irvan and Earnhardt) were side by side going into three," said a happy Earnhardt, who won $87,315.

"I figured somebody would come down and make it three wide coming off (turn) four and then we'd be racing three and four wide and maybe I could sneak on the outside and still beat them. I figured I was going to run second or third.

"Then, Kyle stayed behind me and Mark was behind Ernie, Ernie beat me a little through the trioval and then I stuck it right against him and beat him back by inches.

"We were lucky, just really lucky. All of them were players and all of them were important. You didn't know who was going to push who, or who was going to hurt who. They moved, we moved. It was just an all day game. I just had to play the game until the last move. We got the last move and it worked."

Earnhardt claimed his victory by a mere six inches.

"Dale and I had a heck of a drag race to the finish," Irvan said. "I didn't have anybody on my bumper. That was the problem, but everybody chooses where they want to go and you have to live with it."

Martin finished third, Petty fourth, and Jarrett fifth. Labonte's Ford ran out of gas on the final lap and he had to settle for 15th.

The win was Earnhardt's eighth at Talladega, tying him with the late Davey Allison for the most victories at the circuit's largest speedway. Earnhardt now has six Winston Cup, one Busch Series, and one IROC win at the track. Allison won three Winston Cup, four ARCA and one IROC race at the speedway.

"You can't say enough about Davey and the Allison family," said Earnhardt, who had won five of the last eight Winston Cup races.

"We've mourned Davey for two weeks now. It's been a real tragic thing for the Allison family, but it's like Bobby Allison told Neil a couple nights after that accident, 'You've got to go on and you can't blame yourself for what happened.' Neil tried to do all he could in getting Davey out of that helicopter. You just do what you can and get through what you can get through.

"I think the racing community has pulled together and helped each other get through this trauma with Davey. But you have to go on."

Earnhardt averaged 153.857 mph in the race slowed by five caution flags for 27 laps. There were 26 lead changes among 10 drivers in the race that took 3 hours 15 minutes and 1 second to complete. And Earnhardt said the final 50 laps were tougher than the first 138.

"I knew it was going to be a closer and hotter race (than the first half)," said Earnhardt, who has an average finish of eighth in restrictor plate races, making him the only driver with a top 10 average finish in the restrictor plate events.

"I was more tense right there at the end than I was the whole time."

Earnhardt led five times for 59 laps, while Irvan held the No. 1 spot on six occasions for 56 laps. Petty was the third highest lap leader, setting the pace five times for 39 laps.

"I still shake my head sometimes when I see what Dale Earnhardt does in a race car," said Andy Petree, Earnhardt's crew chief. "It looked like we were going to get beat today, and then the next thing I know, he's out front again. I don't know how he does it, but he seems to always get the job done."

Team owner Richard Childress said he knew Earnhardt's plan when he saw how we was racing on the last lap.

"I've seen him do it before," Childress said. "I had confidence in him. You never know exactly what's going to happen once they go out of sight, but I never lose confidence in Dale." ∎

> ## "I still shake my head sometimes when I see what Dale Earnhardt does in a race car," said Andy Petree, Earnhardt's crew chief.

Earnhardt Victorious At The Rock 63rd Career Win Wraps Up Seventh Winston Cup Title

Earnhardt capped his record-typing seventh Cup championship in style, winning a thrilling last-lap duel with Rick Mast to win the 1994 season finale at North Carolina Speedway. Earnhardt beat Mast by a car length for his fourth win of the season, clinching the championship over Rusty Wallace. His seventh title—his sixth with Richard Childress Racing—matched Richard Petty's record. It would be his final Cup championship.

Dale Earnhardt conquered "The Rock" and NASCAR's Winston Cup circuit all in the same day, winning the AC-Delco 500 by a car length and his record-tying seventh series championship.

The only other driver with seven Winston Cup titles is Richard Petty.

"It's great to be No. 1 all the way around on race day," said an emotional Earnhardt, who dedicated the championship to his best friend, Neil Bonnett, who died in a crash during practice in February at Daytona International Speedway.

"Winston Cup racing is my kind of racing. I wouldn't change a thing."

Earnhardt, who dedicated his race victory to Frank Wilson, the track's president who died in August, now has 63 Winston Cup career victories. The win was his fourth this year and his first since the May 1 Winston Select 500 at Talladega, Ala. It was his second victory at the 1.017-mile track and his first in the fall race.

In the last eight races, Earnhardt has produced one win, three seconds, three thirds and a seventh.

Six of his Winston Cup championships have come with car owner Richard Childress, while his first, in 1980, was with Rod Osterlund.

Earnhardt entered the 492-lap race with a 321-point lead over Rusty Wallace and needed to gain only

50 points to clinch the title. On lap 303, Wallace's championship hopes ended when the engine expired in his Ford and he made that sickening left-hand turn into the garage.

"Well, the championship is over – no doubt about that," said Wallace, who finished 35th and trailed Earnhardt by 448 points with only two races remaining.

"I congratulate Dale Earnhardt on a great job. We just blew too many engines this year. I've got a good engine department and I'm behind 'em. Now it's time to get back and see what's going on."

Earnhardt said he was told Wallace had taken his car behind the wall, but nothing else was said until he won the championship.

"I was just racing like I was before," Earnhardt said. "That's a tough way to go out. I know he's a racer and he's a tough racer and he doesn't want to go out because of broken pieces. There's always next year. That's what

To his competition and many fans, Earnhardt was a blur at Rockingham as he beat the field and clinched his seventh Winston Cup championship.

When you're good, you're good.

you look forward to when the season's over or you end up second. I'm sure it's going to make him more determined."

Even though Earnhardt was the top lap leader, setting the pace on four occasions for 108 laps, he didn't dominate the event and he fought off a strong challenge from Rick Mast in the closing laps.

Earnhardt qualified 20th and didn't take the lead for the first time until lap 173. And even then he led for only one lap, giving himself five bonus points. On lap 173, Earnhardt dove to the inside of leader Ken Schrader, inched ahead of him at the scorer's stand located at the fourth turn exit, but Schrader moved back into the No. 1 spot on lap 174 for 21 laps.

Earnhardt didn't lead again until well after the halfway mark. He inherited the top spot from Terry

Labonte on lap 297 when the Hendrick Motorsports driver made a scheduled green-flag pit stop. Earnhardt led only four laps before he made his green-flag stop.

It took Earnhardt 26 laps to move back to the front, but this time it was his crew who put him into the lead. When Hut Stricklin, Dave Marcis and Mark Martin crashed on the backstretch, the leaders pitted during the five-lap caution period. Earnhardt's crew completed its work first and the No. 3 Chevrolet returned to the track in the lead. This time, Earnhardt led 26 laps, and he only had to deal with Morgan Shepherd and Mast in the final 141 laps. Shepherd set the pace for 33 laps while Mast led 31, but it was all Earnhardt in the final 77.

"I drive a race car 100 percent-plus every race and that's what I intend to do until I retire," Earnhardt said.

With 56 laps remaining, Earnhardt possessed a 2.14-second advantage over Mast, who's still searching for his first career Winston Cup victory. Gradually, Mast began cutting the deficit. On lap 463, when Earnhardt got held up behind the lapped cars of Dale Jarrett and Darrell Waltrip, Mast pulled to within a fraction of a second of Earnhardt.

With 21 laps remaining, Mast closed in on Earnhardt's bumper as they came upon Lake Speed's Ford. On lap 473, Mast stuck the nose of his car to the inside of Earnhardt's Chevrolet but couldn't complete the pass.

Then, on lap 477, Darrell Waltrip's Chevrolet spun and smacked the fourth-turn wall, bringing out the 10th and final caution period. The leaders pitted, but the fresh tires they received helped Earnhardt more than Mast.

"Rick Mast was catching me and he was going to be a factor. I don't know if I could've held him off," Earnhardt said. "My tires were getting loose going into the third turn and I was not able to negotiate that corner as well as I needed to.

"The fresh tires definitely helped us and getting out of the pits first definitely helped us, too."

Mast said it took him 10 to 15 laps after each restart to get his Ford going.

"I caught Earnhardt and I really thought I might have had a shot at passing him, but you know, his bumper gets mighty wide there at the end," Mast said. "Anyhow, when that caution came out there at the end I kind of figured it was over then because I wasn't strong enough for the first five or 10 laps to beat him."

When the race restarted with nine laps remaining, Earnhardt was leading, followed by Mast, Shepherd, Labonte and Ricky Rudd. Earnhardt jumped out to about a 10-car length lead, while Rudd quickly dispensed with Labonte to move into fourth.

On the final lap, Mast went high as they exited turn four and attempted to slingshot low on Earnhardt, but came up a car-length short.

"I eased up on that last corner so I wouldn't make a mistake and Rick almost caught me and got by me," Earnhardt said. "I knew he wanted to win. It would have been his first. I wanted to win, too, and win that championship."

Earnhardt's closest call came on lap 86 during a series of green-flag pit stops. The 43-year-old driver had just ducked onto pit road when Mast and Greg Sacks crashed in turn one. He immediately returned to the track, even though he thought he had a tire going down, so he could remain on the lead lap.

While Earnhardt showed his strength in the race's latter stages, the first half belonged to Geoff Bodine, Mast and Jeff Gordon.

Pole position winner Rudd led the first two laps before Bodine shot underneath him on the backstretch and into the lead for the next 58 laps. The only driver who could stay with Bodine was Mast and, on lap 46, the two had a 3.34-second advantage over third-place Ward Burton.

Mast finally snatched the lead from Bodine on lap 61. He led for 25 laps and was in the top spot when he became squirrelly in turns one and two, slipped into the side of Sacks' Ford and carried the two cars up the track and into the wall. The wreck on lap 86 eliminated Sacks, but Mast's crew worked throughout the race on his damaged Ford.

After Mast's crash, the Hendrick Motorsports stable took command of the event for 209 of the next 211 laps.

"It's great to be No. 1 all the way around on race day." —Earnhardt

It's go time.

During that span, Labonte led on four occasions for 67 laps, Gordon three times for 101 laps and Ken Schrader three times for 41 laps. The only two drivers to lead a lap each during the Hendrick domination were Dick Trickle on lap 163 and Earnhardt 10 laps later.

Schrader's chance at victory ended on lap 221 when the drive shaft came out of his Chevrolet in turns one and two. That piece of debris resulted in Sterling Marlin, Dave Marcis, Ted Musgrave and Jeremy Mayfield crashing as they exited turn two after one of them ran over the drive shaft.

The incident relegated Schrader to a 32nd-place finish.

Gordon's Chevrolet encountered engine problems on lap 226 while running second. On lap 274, he took it to the garage for repairs and returned to the race on lap 307. Gordon salvaged a 29th-place finish.

Even though there were 10 caution flags for 52 laps, there were two incidents that didn't require a yellow flag. One occurred on lap 69 when Steve Grissom's Chevrolet slid off turn four and onto the grassy frontstretch. Grissom kept the car off the track until the traffic had passed and then returned to the race.

The other occurred on lap 121 when Randy MacDonald spun off turn four after being tagged by John Andretti.

Earnhardt averaged 126.407 mph in the final 500-mile race to be held in October at the track. Next year's event will be 400 miles. The race took 3 hours, 57 minutes and 30 seconds to complete. ■

Earnhardt Snatches A Career First

Defending Winston Cup Champion Passes Dominant Martin To Earn Road-Course Win

By the time Earnhardt arrived in Sonoma in 1995, he had nearly done it all. But the Save Mart 300 provided another "first" for the seven-time champion. Always a contender on the road courses, Earnhardt had never emerged from the twisting, winding circuits with a victory. Until now. It was his only career win on the series' serpentine circuits.

Everybody thought this one belonged to Mark Martin, and rightly so.

After all, the driver of the Roush Racing Ford had taken the lead on lap six of the 74-lap Save Mart Supermarkets 300 and was hardly challenged as the event wound to its conclusion.

But instead of a ho-hum tour around the 2.52-mile, 11-turn road course for Martin, the race evolved into something decidedly more dramatic. On lap 73, after several laps of dogged pursuit, Dale Earnhardt took advantage of Martin's slip in a patch of grease in the sweeping sixth turn to take the lead.

From there, Earnhardt powered his RCR Enterprises Chevrolet to the checkered flag to earn his first victory on a road course in his 16-year career, which now spans 490 starts.

"Mark just got into some oil over there in the turn and I got past him," said an elated Earnhardt. "After that, I just wanted to be very careful and not get into trouble, because it was a greasy race track out there.

"We had a car that was very consistent here and that is what we wanted. I could use what I wanted from the car when I wanted it and I can't thank the guys on the crew enough for giving me what I needed."

The victory was the second of the season for Earnhardt, who also won at North Wilkesboro, N.C., in April - the 65th of his career. It was also his 36th career start on a road course with his previous best finish being second, three times.

Earnhardt maintained his lead in the Winston Cup point standings, breaking out of a tie with Jeff Gordon. Earnhardt has 1,494 points, just nine more than Martin, who moved into second place. Gordon, who finished third in the Save Mart Supermarkets 300, fell to third in the points, 15 behind Earnhardt.

Oddly enough, Richard Childress, Earnhardt's team owner, was not around to see his driver score the victory. Seems he was in Africa on a safari.

"Richard told me that I would probably win my first road course race since he was in Africa and wouldn't be around to see it," said Earnhardt, who received $74,860 for the victory. "Well, I got news for him. He's going to Africa instead of the Daytona 500."

Earnhardt has never won the Winston Cup circuit's premier event.

"It's been a goal for me to win on a road course and the Daytona 500," Earnhardt said. "Some things never come to you. But now we've got the road-course win, so we've got that out of the way."

But it didn't come easy. In fact, after pole winner Ricky Rudd gave up his lead after five laps – allowing Martin to whip by him after Rudd missed a shift coming out of turn 11 – the race quickly settled into a Sunday drive for Martin.

The only times Martin surrendered his advantage came when he pitted under green. Following his last pit stop on lap 51, Martin led a trio of himself, Earnhardt and Gordon, all of whom had a comfortable cushion over fourth-place runner Rusty Wallace.

A full-course yellow came out on lap 57 after Hut Stricklin blew an engine in his King Racing Ford. The running order didn't change, it merely tightened when the green flag few on lap 61.

It took less than a lap for another yellow flag to be thrown, and it was for a doozy of a wreck among Wallace, Dale Jarrett and Davy Jones. The three spun in the seventh turn and as a result, Jarrett's Ford came to rest on its right side, eventually to be put back on all four wheels through the efforts of track workers.

Wallace went back to the pits to have sheet metal pulled away from his tires and then returned to the race.

Through all of this, Earnhardt kept his runner-up position, although most of the time, it seemed he was no match for Martin.

"I was just trying to run smooth and consistent," he said. "There were times when the 2 (Wallace) and the 24 (Gordon) would pressure me and that's when I would lose some of what I had. And when I tried to pressure Mark, I would lose it, too.

"We had worked on the shocks and the carburetor before the race, and when it started we seemed to have enough for everybody but Mark. We changed the air pressure a few times and it got better and better. My job was to take the right lines and make sure I stayed on the asphalt."

The race restarted on lap 66 with 29 cars on the lead lap. However, this time Martin could not find the dominance he had held earlier. Earnhardt maintained the pressure, keeping it up for several laps while third-place Gordon began to fall off the pace.

Then, on lap 73, it happened. In the sixth turn of the track area called "The Carousel," Martin slipped high and Earnhardt dove low, taking the lead.

"I smelled rear end grease around turns three, four or five – I don't know which – and I saw a streak of it in turn six when I was on the crest of the hill," Earnhardt said. "My spotter said he thought he saw oil in the turn and there was a car smoking up ahead.

"I moved to the outside and crossed the streak rather than run through it. Mark ran through it and that caused him to slide out. I got inside him and got past him."

After that, Earnhardt's only goal was not to make a mistake and return the lead to Martin.

"I was thinking I had to make a good line and stay on the racing surface and stay out of any oil," Earnhardt said. "I was extra careful in a couple of places and Mark

There aren't many "firsts" left for Earnhardt, but winning his first-ever road course event is one worth celebrating.

"I think I enjoy wins more now in my career than I did earlier." —Earnhardt

came back on me, but I was able to put a few yards on him."

Asked if he felt he could have caught Martin without the presence of grease on the track, Earnhardt said he would have done all he could to win.

"I was going to be on his back bumper and alongside him if I could," Earnhardt said.

Then he added with a smile:

"I was going to race him hard and clean. And by clean, I mean I wasn't going to knock him off the race track…Now why did I say that?

"Mark ran with me at Talladega (on April 30) and he deserved to win that race. He deserved to win this one, too, but we were there when he made the mistake."

Rudd followed the trio of Earnhardt, Martin and Gordon in fourth, suitably recovered from transmission problems in his Ford. Fifth went to Terry Labonte in a Hendrick Chevrolet while Ted Musgrave finished sixth in a Roush Racing Ford. Sterling Marlin took seventh in the Morgan-McClure Chevrolet while Todd Bodine was eighth in the Butch Mock Motorsports Ford, Ken Schrader was ninth in the Hendrick Chevrolet and Michael Waltrip completed the top 10 in the Bahari Racing Pontiac.

While Wallace ran as high as third, he pitted under the race's fourth caution period – caused by Stricklin's engine problems – along with Jarrett, and thus was put in the wrong place at the wrong time. His crash with Jarrett and Jones in the seventh turn helped relegate him to 20th place.

It was a circumstance similar to Earnhardt's a week ago at Talladega, where he was in the wrong place at the wrong time. A last-lap altercation with Morgan Shepherd sent him from a possible third-place finish to 21st. That resulted in the tie with Gordon for first place in the point standings coming into Sears Point.

"What happened last week just happened last week," answered Earnhardt when asked if his Sonoma victory made up for the disappointing Talladega finish. "It is over and done with. That is the way this team treats it. We race one week and go on to the next race."

As for road racing, Earnhardt admits he feels somewhat vindicated.

"I have always thought I was a good road racer," he said. "I've won poles here and at Watkins Glen (the other road course on the Winston Cup circuit). I've had good cars here, too. But I never seemed to be around at the finish. I would tear up transmissions or rear ends or something.

"But I don't really think this win is any more special than any other. They are all special. I think I enjoy wins more now in my career than I did earlier. They just don't seem to come quick enough for me. But I consider myself fortunate to be able to have some wins after all these years in racing."

And with this one, perhaps all that is left is the big one in Daytona. ∎

Dale Takes Second-Ever Brickyard

Earnhardt Beats Old Rival To Gain Indy Glory

Winning the second NASCAR race ever held at the Indianapolis Motor Speedway marked Earnhardt's only victory at the famed oval. He led the final 27 laps of the race, whose inaugural event was won by Earnhardt rival Jeff Gordon. Considering he had not won a Daytona 500, winning the Cup race at Indianapolis ranked among the biggest moments in Earnhardt's career.

The Brickyard 400 is a new race on the Winston Cup circuit, but its exciting finish had an old, familiar ring to it.

Dale Earnhardt, the defending Winston Cup champion whose name has recently dropped out of the headlines as Jeff Gordon has become the darling of the stock car world, held off old rival Rusty Wallace – another whose fortunes have not been good lately – and a charging Dale Jarrett to win the second running of the Brickyard 400.

In a thrilling conclusion to what was an extraordinarily long day at the 2.5-mile Indianapolis oval, Earnhardt beat Wallace to the checkered flag by 0.426 second to win his third race of the season and

his first since he won on the road course at Sears Point Raceway in early May.

Since then, Earnhardt's best run had been a third in the Pepsi 400 at Daytona Beach, Fla. He had suffered three finishes of 20th or worse and drifted as far back as fourth in the Winston Cup point standings, which he led through much of the first six months of the season. After the Dover, Del., race in June, he was atop the standings by 100 points, but he was in third place, 146 points behind Gordon, when the Indy race began.

The Brickyard 400 was one race Earnhardt desperately wanted to win, especially after he whacked the first-turn wall on the first lap of last year's race and

Earnhart likes holding the BIG checks.

No. 000001

NET AMOUNT

$200,000.00

ultimately had to settle for a fifth-place finish.

The only other race as coveted by Earnhardt is the Daytona 500, which he has never won.

"This is a neat deal," an excited Earnhardt said from victory lane. "I've never won the Daytona 500, but the Brickyard 400 is a special race. It's right next to Daytona, so I'll take it. Hey, only two of us have won this race."

Earnhardt was referring to Gordon, the winner of the inaugural Indy race who has gone on to win five times this year and take the lead in the point standings – and be something of a thorn in Earnhardt's side.

"I can't thank (team owner) Richard Childress and all the guys back in the shop enough," said Earnhardt, who now has 66 career victories. "We put a new Chevrolet together for this race and got in only about 40 laps of practice, and then we go out and win.

"We made changes to the car all week and we made changes to it this morning, to tell the truth. But

> **"Well, it's not as much [money] as Jeff [Gordon] won last year, so I guess I can't afford to go to Disneyland," Earnhardt said. "I guess I'll have to go to Opryland."**

our car and crew are hard to beat when they're on, and they were on today."

When the day began, it appeared the race was certain to be rained out. The residue of Hurricane Erin enveloped Indianapolis and the race's planned starting time of 1:15 p.m. EDT came and went with fans, officials, crewmen and drivers seeking shelter from the weather.

As bleak as the prospects were, by 4:25 p.m. the green flag fell, with many fans who had departed speedway grounds scrambling to return to their seats. The last time a race was delayed at Indianapolis came in 1991, when the Indianapolis 500 started 55 minutes late.

Pole winner Gordon, who took qualifying honors on Aug. 3 before the second round of time trials was rained out, quickly pulled away. In his bid to win a second straight Brickyard 400, he led until lap 31, when he pitted. He obviously didn't know it at the time, but he would lead only four more laps.

The race was then dominated by some of NASCAR's top veterans. Bill Elliott, another driver whose fortunes haven't been the best lately, led the majority of laps as the first 100 circuits of the 160-lapper were completed.

On lap 109, Wallace took the lead when he passed Gordon's Hendrick Chevrolet in the first turn. Wallace would lead through lap 128, when he pitted under green. Earnhardt had pitted a lap earlier. He was thus able to take track position ahead of Wallace, whose cause was not helped when he was forced to check up on pit road after Joe Nemechek cut in front of Rich Bickle and clipped Bickle's Pontiac.

During a series of green-flag stops, John Andretti inherited the lead on lap 130.

Then, on lap 132, the first caution period of the race was created when Jeff Burton spun coming out of the second turn in front of Earnhardt, who escaped. Burton's car then crossed Wallace's path and nearly hit him.

Andretti pitted and the quick work done earlier by Earnhardt's RCR Enterprises put the seven-time Winston Cup champion in front when the green flag fell on lap 137. Wallace was second, followed by Elliott, Jarrett and Gordon.

"That last stop was the key," Earnhardt said. "We got out in front of Rusty and that was the key to the win. When the race restarted, I had all the clean air out front."

Earnhardt would not give up his lead throughout the final 27 laps. Wallace tried hard to overtake him – and on occasion seemed to be in position to do so – but could not.

"At the end, I put pressure on myself to drive hard, be consistent and not make a mistake," Earnhardt said. "I was out front with the clean air and that worked well for me. I wasn't worried about Rusty, although if he got under me he would be trouble. But he had to be the one to make a move and do whatever he could do. I just had to stay consistent. I was going to drive my line and keep my line and not worry about it."

Meanwhile, Jarrett, who had started 26th, used the handling and power of his Ford to its best advantage. He chased Elliott down and then passed him on lap 149 in the third turn to take third place.

The finish evolved into an Earnhardt-Wallace-Jarrett chase. By lap 154, they had built a substantial lead over fourth-place Elliott, who was having to lift a sticking brake pedal with his foot.

Earnhardt withstood the challenge.

"I was better out front than I was behind," Earnhardt said. "When I got behind, it pushed. It just wouldn't go as good. When I got out front, it was real good. That's where I wanted to be.

"We beat 'em out on that last green-flag stop, so we had track position when that caution period started. The 8 car (Burton) wrecked in front of us. He clipped me a little bit and sort of spun me a little bit and got me real loose, but we recovered from that. And so, we were out front. We had the track position."

Wallace, who has won only once this year – after compiling 18 victories in 1993-94 – scored his best finish since his victory at Martinsville, Va., in April.

Jarrett, another driver whose fortunes were sour until he won at Pocono three races ago, kept his streak going. He now has a victory, a runner-up finish and a third-place run in the last three events. And Elliott's fourth-place finish was his best of the season.

Martin finished fifth, followed by Gordon, Sterling Marlin, Rick Mast, Bobby Labonte and Morgan Shepherd.

Gordon held on to first place in the point standings. He has 2,860 points, 82 more than Marlin. Earnhardt remained third, now 121 points behind.

By being the points leader after the Indy race, Gordon collected a $100,000 bonus for the second time this year. The first came after the Winston Select 500 at Talladega, Ala., in April. His earnings for the race totaled $299,200.

For winning, Earnhardt took home $565,600, just a little less than Gordon received last year.

"Well, it's not as much as Jeff won last, year, so I guess I can't afford to go to Disneyland," Earnhardt said. "I guess I'll have to go to Opryland."

Earnhardt put much more emphasis on the victory than could be provided by money alone.

First, he won at Indy.

"To come here and to race here is a big honor and experience," he said. "And to finish fifth in the first race was a great accomplishment as far as I was concerned.

"But to win at the same track where a Rick Mears, or the Unsers or all those other great names have won, to have your name in the same group of names of drivers who have won an Indy 500 or a Brickyard 400, that is pretty impressive."

And to once again have your name on everyone's lips has its merits, too, although Earnhardt is not about to criticize Gordon – the driver who has clearly stolen the Winston Cup thunder in 1995.

"Do you think I need to reestablish myself?" he responded when asked if his Indy victory did just that. "Do you think people have forgotten me? I don't think I need to reestablish myself. I just needed to win again.

"I'm not going to take anything away from Jeff, his talents or his team. His future is bright. He's a great racer who is due all the press and the reputation he's got. But there have been a lot of others who have come along before him."

The victory also provided Earnhardt with a forum to declare that he and his team are not ready to be counted out, despite the downward shift in the point standings or attention given anyone else.

"I've overheard comments that the 3 team is under pressure and is pulling at each other while the 24 team (Gordon's) is laid back," Earnhardt said. "Our guys are confident and hard-working. As a team they pull together and don't give up. They don't feel under pressure even when we're behind Gordon and Marlin in points.

"You're not going to beat us by talking about us. You've got to beat us on the track."

And on a long day at Indianapolis, no one could do that. ■

Teresa takes a moment to congratulate Dale.

Elation erupts in victory lane as Earnhardt takes to the roof of his GM Goodwrench Chevrolet to celebrate his capture of the one title that has eluded him – The Daytona 500.

At Last
Earnhardt Finally Bags The Big One

For 20 years, Dale Earnhardt had won every race imaginable at famed Daytona International Speedway—except the big one, the Daytona 500. Earnhardt, who had lost the race every way imaginable, finally won it in 1998, snapping a 51-race winless streak. "Twenty years. Can you believe it?" Earnhardt said. "The monkey is off my back." Earnhardt's biggest win sparked an emotional celebration, one that included the crews of nearly every team lining pit road to congratulate him. It was his record 31st victory in all divisions at Daytona, a track he had mastered even before winning the 500.

It evolved into a cloudy, gray day. But for Dale Earnhardt, it was the brightest of his career. Who needed the sun?

At last ... at last.

In one of the most emotion-charged finishes in the history of Daytona, Earnhardt, a seven-time Winston Cup champion whose racing achievements are the stuff of dreams, did something he hadn't been able to do for 20 years. He won the Daytona 500 – finally.

Now, as Earnhardt put it, "The monkey is off my back!" And he so exuberantly illustrated that fact by hurling a stuffed monkey across the press box.

With the victory, Earnhardt removed the one stigma of his celebrated career. No longer can it be said that Earnhardt, one of the greatest drivers in NASCAR history, can't win the Daytona 500.

And no longer will he be bothered by the question, "When will you win the Daytona 500?"

"Yes! Yes! Yes!" said an excited Earnhardt in victory lane. "Twenty years! Can you believe it!"

Believe it. After years in which Earnhardt lost the Daytona 500 in just about every way imaginable – out of gas here, a cut tire there, a missing lug nut over there – this time fate would not deny him.

Earnhardt, who has now won 31 races at Daytona including this first Daytona 500, also ended a 59-race losing streak and effectively hushed the talk that he could no longer drive 500 hard, competitive miles – talk that intensified after he mysteriously blacked out on the first lap of the Southern 500 at Darlington last year.

He was clearly the sentimental favorite in Daytona. Even those who do not count themselves among his fans said that if their chosen driver could not win, they wanted Earnhardt to win to end his years of futility.

Now, as Earnhardt put it, "The monkey is off my back!" And he so exuberantly illustrated that fact by hurling a stuffed monkey across the press box.

And wouldn't victory for the long-suffering Earnhardt be a perfect fit for NASCAR's year-long 50th Anniversary celebration?

"This win is for all our fans and all the people who told me, 'Dale, this is your year,'" Earnhardt said. "I mean, you can't believe all the people who told me that, from the top to the bottom in the garage area. Team owners to crewmen. Bill France. Todd Parrott (Dale Jarrett's crew chief).

"There was a lot of hard work that went into this and I have to thank every member of the Richard Childress Racing team. I have had a lot of great fans and people behind me all through the years and I just can't thank them enough.

"The Daytona 500 is over. And we won it! We won it!"

But he very easily could have lost it – again – and if he had, it would have gone down as one of the most disappointing episodes of his career.

As it turned out, Earnhardt held off a furious attack from the likes of Jeremy Mayfield, Rusty Wallace and Bobby Labonte as the 200-lap race around the 2.5-mile Daytona track sped to its conclusion.

Earnhardt, in a Chevrolet, was the race's dominant figure. But as he himself will tell you, that's never been enough in itself for him to win the Daytona 500. This time, it was.

Earnhardt, who led five times for 107 laps, more than any other driver, made a pass around teammate Mike Skinner on lap 140 to take the lead he would hold for the remainder of the race, although he certainly didn't know it at the time.

On lap 174, the race's second caution period began after Robert Pressley and John Andretti spun down the backstretch. One lap later, Earnhardt led the parade of leaders down pit road.

It was obvious that this would be the final stop and the leaders opted to make it as quick as possible. With the exception of Ernie Irvan, all took on right side tires only.

"We had learned from the 125-mile qualifying race that track position was very important," said Larry McReynolds, Earnhardt's crew chief who had won Daytona 500s in 1992 with Davey Allison and in 1996 with Jarrett. "We knew what all the other teams were thinking and to us, there was no question to go for just two tires. In fact, Goodyear brought such a good tire here we might have been OK if we just took gas.

"We knew it would take five or six seconds to take fuel and the guys made about an 8.5-second stop for tires and that let us get back out on the track first."

"On the last stop, I was focused," Earnhardt said. "I wanted to make sure I didn't do anything wrong and that we got out quick. And we did."

Earnhardt was followed by Skinner, Mayfield, Wallace and Jeff Gordon, the winner of the 1997 Daytona 500.

When the race restarted, there were just 12 laps to go. Earnhardt was in front with teammate Skinner behind him. That gave Earnhardt the ideal drafting partner and he would need it, because in third and fourth were Mayfield and Wallace, who became teammates in the Penske organization this season when Roger Penske became a partner with Michael Kranefuss on Mayfield's team.

It was clear Earnhardt and Skinner would combine their forces to escape Mayfield and Wallace, if they could.

Earnhardt glued a lucky penny to his dash before the 500.

"Mike did help a tremendous amount on that last restart," Earnhardt said. "I know he would have liked to have won this race as much as me."

But the strategy was doomed. On lap 179, Skinner was pushed high out of the draft in turn one and that allowed Mayfield and Wallace, in Fords, to close on Earnhardt's rear bumper. Gordon moved to fourth place and Skinner fought Labonte for fifth.

Five laps passed as Earnhardt, now on his own, eyed his rearview mirror and kept his foot in the throttle as the Penske Fords lurked just behind.

"I felt like I could do pretty good, but Jeremy and Rusty were hooked up good," Earnhardt said. "I don't know, but I just felt like this was it."

On lap 184, Gordon shot to the low side of Wallace in the first turn, but Wallace made a blocking move that broke his effort with Mayfield and allowed Earnhardt some precious space.

On lap 194, Gordon made another move. This time he went to the high side of the Fords ahead of him and split them, moving into third place behind Mayfield.

The running order stayed that way until lap 197, when Wallace shot by Gordon on the backstretch and once again united with his teammate.

Then, one lap later, pole-winner Labonte pushed his Pontiac to the high side and managed to clear Mayfield coming out of the fourth turn to move into second place. As he did so, Gordon drifted back out of the melee, the victim of a dropped cylinder.

There were two laps remaining.

On lap 199, the race's third and final caution period began when Andretti, Lake Speed and Jimmy Spencer tangled on the backstretch. When the leaders got back to the line, they would see the yellow and white flags fly simultaneously.

The first one to the flags would win the race.

Earnhardt gave it all he had. He was able to utilize the lapped Ford of Rick Mast as a pick and got a bit of a break as Labonte and Mayfield jostled each other for position.

He crossed the line ahead of them. And the grandstands erupted.

One last, comfortable, tension-free lap was all Earnhardt had left to make. With the checkered flag came the end of 19 years of frustration.

"We worked awful hard and just kept playing our cards," said Earnhardt, 46. "They'd go this way and I'd go with them or do what I thought was best. The years of experience helped me out there.

"I was hoping they would stay in line with about 10 to go or eight to go. It got down to five and they got to racing. They started dicing and that made me feel better. I could pick who I wanted to dice with as they were passing each other.

"When Bobby got in behind me, he was pretty much by himself. He didn't have any help. And we had Rick's lapped car there. I felt like I could hold him off."

Earnhardt admitted he got emotional as he sped past the yellow and white flags.

"My eyes watered up in the race car," he said. "I don't think I really cried. My eyes just watered up on that lap to take the checkered. I knew I was going to win it then, no matter what. I knew I was going to win unless something happened to the car.

"I was driving slow down the backstretch and I said, 'I want to go fast. I don't want to go slow. I want to get back around there.' I took off, came back around, took the checkered and really got excited."

By his own admission, what happened next will be forever etched in Earnhardt's memory. As he made his way down pit road toward victory lane, he was met by crew members from virtually every team in the Daytona 500, all of whom wanted to congratulate him for his victory.

"I sorta expected a few of them to come out there, but not as many as there were," Earnhardt said. "All the guys came up congratulating me, all of them wanting to shake my hand or give me high-fives, thumbs-up. There was Michael Waltrip, Rusty ... I had to go real slow or my arm would've gotten torn off."

As if to display his excitement to the fans, Earnhardt sped off pit road, into the grass and cut doughnuts with his spinning tires. Later, fans would retrieve chunks of the torn-up sod for souvenirs.

The victory was worth $1,059,105 to Earnhardt and marked the first time in Winston Cup racing the winner's share of the purse was over $1 million. He won with an average speed of 172.712 mph, the third-fastest race in Daytona 500 history.

"I had confidence in myself, the team and everybody," Earnhardt said. "People say, 'Did you hear things? Did you wonder who was going to pass?' I was working to keep the race car out in front. I was working to do that until somebody turned me over or we got to the finish.

"I wasn't thinking about what could happen. I was thinking about what I was doing and focused on what I had to do."

Labonte wound up second, Mayfield third and Ken Schrader, broken sternum and all, came home fourth. Wallace was fifth, with Ernie Irvan sixth, Chad Little seventh, Skinner eighth, Michael Waltrip ninth and Bill Elliott 10th.

Earnhardt now is eligible for a $1 million bonus from Winston in the No Bull 5 program. He joined the other top-five finishers, Labonte, Mayfield, Schrader and Wallace, as candidates for the reward if any one of them can win the Coca-Cola 600 at Charlotte on May 24.

While Earnhardt would be the first to tell you he wouldn't turn down a $1 million bonus, he's out for greater rewards.

"Another championship is going to make it complete," he said. "Honestly, I'm telling you this and not because we won the race, but because we've got a race team. We have guys who are ready to win races. We are going to concentrate on winning the eighth championship."

And now, there is no longer any need to concentrate on that first Daytona 500 win after coming so excruciatingly close over the years. Earnhardt ran out of gas to lose to Geoff Bodine in 1986. Then there was the now-famous cut tire on the last lap in 1990 that passed the win to Derrike Cope. Three times in the last five years he has finished second.

Today, he was second to no one.

"It was my time," Earnhardt said. "That's all I can say. I've been passed here. I've run out of gas. I've been cut down with a tire. I've done it all.

"I wrote the book and this is the last chapter in this book. I'm going to start a new book next year. It's over with.

"Every which way you can lose it, I've lost it. Now I've won it and I don't care how I won it. We won it."

At last. ∎

Earnhardt's satisfaction shines brighter than any trophy.

Still The Man

Earnhardt Flashes Championship Form In Dominating Victory

When Dale Earnhardt arrived at Talladega Superspeedway in April 1999, it didn't matter that he had won only one points race since the spring of 1996. He was the master of restrictor-plate racing and at his best at Talladega. He returned to form in the DieHard 500, leading 70 of 188 laps and holding off Dale Jarrett to win by 0.137 second. "He's the master of restrictor-plate racing. He's the best I've ever come up against," third-place Mark Martin said. The win came after violent crashes there in 1996 and '98. "[The crash] in '96 broke me up pretty good, and '98 burned me up pretty good," Earnhardt said. He avoided the melee in 1999 and conquered the track for the ninth time in his career.

The night before the DieHard 500, when Dale Earnhardt unveiled his new car for next month's The Winston all-star race, a crowd of about 100 rabid fans flocked to the International Motorsports Hall of Fame to see their hero in person.

As Earnhardt and car owner Richard Childress took the stage and took the wraps off their special Wrangler-sponsored car, the noise was deafening as the fans whooped, hooted and hollered, undaunted by the fact that Earnhardt had visited victory lane in Winston Cup just once since the spring of 1996 and hadn't led a single lap so far in 1999.

"You're still the man, Dale!" they yelled, over and over and over again, with a fervor that bordered on evangelism.

In the DieHard 500, the seven-time NASCAR Winston Cup champion proved those fans right, at least for one day.

For on this muggy Alabama afternoon, Earnhardt was indeed still the man – "The Intimidator," "The Dominator," "The Man In Black," all rolled into one. Maybe he won't flash this form at the next race, or the race after that, but today he looked like a man with 72 career Winston Cup wins, seven titles and eight career victories at the circuit's fastest and most dangerous track.

This wasn't the Earnhardt who was hurt here in 1996 and '98 when he ended up on his roof in two horrifying wrecks. Instead, this was the man who left the rest of the field fighting for second place, the man who inspired such phenomenal fan loyalty and passion.

This was the Earnhardt people remembered and he made one thing absolutely certain: No one is tougher to pass at the end of a restrictor-plate race.

"I want to tell you guys something," car owner Richard Childress would say after the DieHard 500. "People came up and asked if Dale Earnhardt was too

Earnhardt celebrates his 72nd career victory, following a dominating performance in the DieHard 500 at Talladega. It was only Earnhardt's second win since 1996.

"I had a couple of different reporters ask me if I thought Dale was past his prime. I think today should answer a lot of those questions." —Richard Childress

busy to win races. I had a couple of different reporters ask me if I thought Dale was past his prime. I think today should answer a lot of those questions."

Talladega Superspeedway is a track where you can always count on something happening, typically a 200-mph wreck that takes out half the field.

Earnhardt had been in two of them in the last three years, in fact.

"(The crash) in '96 broke me up pretty good and '98 burned me up pretty good," Earnhardt said. "It's a tough track to race on. Crashes happen and it gets serious. A lot of metal is coming at you."

And so the day began with a mixture of dread and anticipation, waiting to see what would occur in 188 laps of high-speed restrictor-plate racing.

The weirdness began early. Real early, in fact.

On the very first warm-up lap, Winston Cup points leader Jeff Burton's Roush Racing Ford began blowing huge plumes of thick white smoke out of its headers and he was forced into the pits. He went back out and rejoined the field at the tail of the pack, his car still smoking heavily, though it mysteriously stopped and he was able to continue.

When the green flag fell to start the race, Bobby Labonte muscled by pole-sitter Ken Schrader to assume the lead on the first lap, a spot he held until Wally Dallenbach went high in turn two to take the lead on lap six.

By this time, Earnhardt already had moved from his 17th starting spot all the way to third, and from there he would pass both Jeff Gordon and Dallenbach on lap 11

to move into the lead, the first of seven times he would hold the top spot.

Already, the madness was starting, with clusters of drivers running three- and four-wide, jockeying for position and looking for all the world like the only question would be when the 20-car pile-up would happen, not if it would happen.

Over the first 49 laps, the lead changed hands seven times among Earnhardt, Bobby Labonte, Dallenbach, Mike Skinner, Tony Stewart and John Andretti.

Predictably, whenever the cars went three-wide, someone would lose the lead draft and fall far back into the pack. It happened to Skinner once, dropping him from fourth to 15th in a single lap. It would later happen to Andretti and Labonte as well, and even once or twice to Earnhardt.

With all the dicing for position, sooner or later somebody was going to make a mistake. A big one.

This year's edition of the big crash occurred on lap 49, when Skinner led Stewart as both dove down near the grass on the backstretch. Stewart's Pontiac tapped the rear of Skinner's Chevrolet, sending it spinning into the middle of the pack, where it was struck by Jeff Gordon's Chevrolet. As Gordon's Chevrolet careened helplessly toward the top of the backstretch, it was nailed by Rusty Wallace's Ford and Ernie Irvan's Pontiac.

Also caught up in the melee were Chad Little, Kenny Irwin and Dallenbach.

On the ensuing pit stops on lap 54, Ward Burton and Johnny Benson collided on pit road. Burton got the worst of it, his right front heavily damaged, though both stayed in the race.

It could have been a lot worse. This time, only eight cars were involved and no one was hurt, though there were plenty of bad tempers and finger-pointing afterward, as there always are.

When the clean up was completed and the track went green again on lap 58, Earnhardt was fourth, trailing leader Andretti and Bobby and Terry Labonte.

It only took one lap for Earnhardt to put his familiar black No. 3 Chevrolet back in front, going three-wide with Andretti and Michael Waltrip, who would run near the front all day before fading late to finish 18th.

Waltrip, in fact, assumed the lead on lap 68, going high on the backstretch to take the lead, a lead he would hold until near the race's midpoint. On lap 92, Jarrett took the lead for the first time, though only for one lap until Earnhardt sailed past him on the backstretch. They swapped places again on lap 101, with Jarrett taking the lead in turn three.

The leaders all pitted under green on lap 109, with first Schrader and then Jeremy Mayfield taking the lead, while Earnhardt dropped briefly to eighth as he opted for four fresh tires while Schrader and a couple of other drivers only took two.

Earnhardt was back in front on lap 120, a position he would hold for 15 laps until the day's second caution for Terry Labonte's spin in turn four.

When the leaders pitted on lap 135, Earnhardt's day took what looked like an irreversible turn for the worse.

His crew changed four tires and inspected the right front for a suspected vibration.

"We took a little extra time," Earnhardt explained. "Everything looked good, so we came out a little further back than we wanted to, but we had the race car to come back to the front."

Boy did he ever.

When Earnhardt rejoined the race, he was all the way back in 16th place, with barely 50 laps to go. But he made up ground in a hurry. The green flag flew on lap 140, and Earnhardt charged to sixth by lap 145, and third behind Andretti and Waltrip just one lap later. On lap 147 he eased into second and on 148, he went high into turn three as leader Andretti lost the draft and dropped from first to seventh in the blink of an eye.

Just like that, the black Chevrolet with the No. 3 on the side was out front.

"Everybody was pretty racy," Earnhardt said. "I wanted to get to the second or third position so I could work my way to the front or have the opportunity to race for the win."

That he did, but not without a fight.

On lap 151, Waltrip took the lead, only to be overtaken the very next time around by Bobby Labonte.

Then it started getting wild again. Jarrett went high in turn two on lap 163, taking Earnhardt with him into second past Labonte, who promptly repassed Earnhardt the next lap.

As the laps dwindled down, three-wide running became the norm, with drivers sometimes going

"Trying to pass Dale Earnhardt at one of these restrictor-plate tracks with two or three laps to go is a pretty tall order," said Jarrett. "He makes the No. 3 car pretty wide."

Lest you forget why he's "The Intimidator."

even four- and five-wide in a restrictor-plate free-for-all.

For a time, it looked as though Jarrett's Robert Yates Racing Ford, the car which had won here last October, might have the measure of Earnhardt. But the last of the race's three cautions flew on lap 170 when Bobby Hamilton and Robert Pressley wrecked in turn one.

Earnhardt, who had been strong on restarts all day, wasted no time. The green flew on lap 174, and the leaders went three-wide on the backstretch, with Earnhardt going under Andretti to take second in turn three.

Then he and Andretti passed Jarrett on the backstretch on lap 175.

And once Earnhardt is out front on a restrictor-plate track with only 13 laps to go, he is not an easy man to pass, though everyone tried. Labonte and Stewart worked with Mark Martin, who hadn't been much of a factor all day. Jarrett gave it all he had, too.

With nine laps to go it was Earnhardt ahead of Andretti, Mayfield, Jarrett, Schrader and Martin. With six to go, Jarrett was back up to third and two laps later, the luckless Andretti was hung out and headed for a ninth-place finish.

"I knew something was going to happen," Earnhardt said. "The 88 (Jarrett) got a run on the 43 (Andretti) and he wasn't going to sit there. He wanted to be behind me or in front of me. When he made that move, I countered, and that made the decision that the 88 was going to be the better car. It worked out for us. It was a game of chess, knowing when to move and where to move to, and I can't play chess."

Oh, yes he could. And he did.

Earnhardt and Jarrett began to pull away, with Martin joining the fray two laps from the end.

"They got to racing so much there behind us, it allowed Jarrett and I to run our laps," Earnhardt said. "I didn't know if it would last until the end or they would mount a charge and a string would come back. Mark did break away and Mark came to the back of Jarrett in the last lap.

"It was a little too late and Jarrett couldn't make a move to run on me. It was fortunate it worked out that way and there wasn't any more laps left. They would have probably got to me and got by me."

But at the end of the day, the only thing the two Ford drivers had for Earnhardt was praise.

"Trying to pass Dale Earnhardt at one of these restrictor-plate tracks with two or three laps to go is a pretty tall order," said Jarrett. "He makes the No. 3 car pretty wide."

"He's sort of the master of restrictor-plate racing," agreed Martin. "He's the best I've ever come up against."

And that's how the DieHard 500 ended: Earnhardt winning by 0.137 second over Jarrett and Martin, after leading a race-high 70 of 188 laps.

The Joe Gibbs Racing Pontiac teammates Labonte and Stewart were fourth and fifth, respectively, followed by another pair of teammates, the Andy Petree Racing duo of Schrader and Kenny Wallace. Rounding out the top 10 were Jerry Nadeau in the Melling Racing Ford, Andretti and Bill Elliott.

Needless to say, it was a big day for Earnhardt, Childress and Kevin Hamlin, who earned his first Winston Cup win as a crew chief, after plenty of frustrations and a couple of near-misses.

"We've been real close, but in this sport, you can't just be close, you've got to be right on," Hamlin said. "We're really working hard with the cars and the pit crews, the whole package. Hopefully we can carry some of this momentum forward."

Earnhardt is sure the team can and he's looking ahead to the May 2 California 500.

"We've got a brand-new car for California and if it doesn't go fast it'll be my fault because the car is really good," he said. "We've had a real crappy year so far, but I think it's going to turn around for us. We've got some good race cars coming out now. We've got a lot of things going on that are going to get better as we go."

Although it's hard to image how they could get much better than they were at Talladega. ∎

Earnhardt slips past a spinning and fuming Terry Labonte after "bumping" him on the final lap. Labonte crashed into the inside wall while Earnhardt took the checkered flag.

"Ironhead" vs. "Iron Man"

Earnhardt Pushes Way To Controversial Last-Lap Win At Bristol

Maybe the only victory where Earnhardt could hear the chorus of boos from the stands, Earnhardt dumped Terry Labonte between turns 1 and 2 for the victory. While fans celebrated Earnhardt's aggressive nature, this time he appeared to have gone too far. Labonte pledged to retaliate in the future against Earnhardt, who in typical Earnhardt fashion was unrepentant for the accident and said he didn't turn Labonte intentionally.

Surreal. Absolutely surreal. Wrecked race cars littered across the track as the checkered flag flies, outrageous controversy, screaming and finger-flipping fans teetering on the edge of delirium, angry race teams and a race no one will soon forget.

In other words, just another typical August Saturday night at Bristol Motor Speedway, deja vu all over again.

Tempers run hot and out of control at the high-banked 0.533-mile Bristol pressure cooker, a place where you damn well better be ready to fight if you come.

And in the entire half century history of NASCAR, you can make a pretty compelling case that no one's ever spoiled for a fight more than seven-time champion Dale Earnhardt.

Call him "The Man In Black," "The Intimidator," "Ironhead" or what you choose, no one has a stronger will to win than Earnhardt. And while some were ready to dismiss the 48-year-old, Kannapolis, N.C., native as being over the hill after a winless 1997 season and just one victory last year, Earnhardt proved he's far from finished at this year's running of the Goody's Headache Powder 500 in Bristol.

In fact, Earnhardt laid waste to the old adage about not teaching old dogs new tricks, 'cause he sure learned an important one here:

Earnhardt pops the cork on his second win of the season.

You can't win wrecking Terry Labonte in the last turn of the last lap, as he did in 1995. To win, you've got to wreck him in the first turn of the last lap.

Four years ago at Bristol, Earnhardt rammed the back of Labonte coming out of turn four, but the Texan's mangled Hendrick Motorsports Chevrolet still managed to slide across the finish line first with Earnhardt second.

This time was different. Tonight, before God, country, a full moon and 141,000 fired up race fans, Earnhardt again popped Labonte, this time between turns one and two of lap 500, igniting a firestorm of rage among rivals and race fans alike and relegating Labonte to eighth, after he had made a miraculous late charge and seemed certain of victory.

Finishing between the victorious Earnhardt and the vanquished Labonte were Jimmy Spencer, Ricky Rudd, Jeff Gordon, Tony Stewart, Mark Martin and Sterling Marlin in seventh. Rounding out the top 10 were Ward Burton and Ken Schrader.

It was Earnhardt's second win of the season, ninth at Bristol and 73rd overall of his illustrious career. And while Earnhardt and the Richard Childress Racing team were happy, few others were. The fans roared their collective discontent, ringing the track with obscenities, upraised middle fingers and choruses of boos. Many competitors were angry afterward as well.

"It wasn't right. It wasn't right," second-place finisher Jimmy Spencer said of Earnhardt's roughhouse tactics. Spencer, himself no stranger to aggressive driving, said, "I used to fight for stuff worse than that on Saturday nights."

"To tell you the truth, I knew there was going to be a wreck," added Rudd. " ... In that situation, you've got to look at who you're dealing with."

Earnhardt, as you might expect, was unapologetic.

"If it comes down to the last lap and you're going for it and you get into somebody, you get into them. You don't mean to, but you mean to race them."

The chaotic finish led NASCAR officials to huddle for more than hour before letting the victory stand.

Well after midnight, NASCAR Chief Operating Officer Mike Helton stood outside the NASCAR trailer trying to explain why Earnhardt's victory was allowed to stand despite the hard contact that sent Labonte into the wall.

"After seeing the end of the race and reviewing all of the tapes, NASCAR is going to let the finish order stand as it completed," Helton said.

"Naturally it would have been better had the race finished under different circumstances, but inasmuch as in having to make a decision whether or not you take a race away from someone for something that happens on the race track, the information that you have or the result is, you have to be very inconclusive and be certain about that. And in this case it's not inconclusive that it was a racing accident on the way back to the checkered flag. And therefore we're going to leave the standings the way they were at the finish of the race.

"If there were going to be any actions taken, they would have been taken tonight. Whether or not NASCAR takes a look at future steps to avoid these types of incidents in the past that are not clearly handled, we may take a look at that, but tonight's results will stand the way they are."

Earnhardt, who has seen both sides of bump-and-run moves over the years, shrugged off the criticism.

"I've always just took my medicine, took what happened and just sucked it up and just go to the next race. You can't change or do anything about it," he said.

Labonte, naturally was unimpressed.

"I won't even waste my time to go to the (NASCAR) trailer and talk to them about it. I've been there before."

And he was none too subtle about giving Earnhardt a payback.

"He better tighten his belts," warned Labonte.

"It wasn't right. It wasn't right," second-place finisher Jimmy Spencer said of Earnhardt's roughhouse tactics.

It didn't take long for the action to heat up. Second-qualifier Rusty Wallace grabbed the lead from pole-sitter Stewart at the start, powering around the outside of the Joe Gibbs Racing Pontiac when the green flag dropped.

Hapless Robert Pressley was the first casualty of the Saturday night bullring madness, wrecking his Jasper Motorsports Ford between turns one and two on lap three to bring out the first caution of the night.

Although he lost the lead at the start, Stewart hounded Wallace and on lap 22 popped him in the rear bumper between turns three and four just to let him know he was still there.

On lap 27, Stewart finally made it by Wallace, taking over the point off of turn two, a move Gordon would repeat a lap later to drop Wallace to third place.

Up front, Stewart held on comfortably, with the order of the top three staying the same for the next 50 laps.

Then came the first key moment of the race.

On lap 78 points leader Dale Jarrett got squirrelly off of turn two, and as the parade of Cup cars made their way to three, all hell broke loose as Jarrett spun and collected John Andretti, Hut Stricklin, Michael Waltrip, Bill Elliott, Jeremy Mayfield and Bobby Hamilton.

Although Jarrett suffered only right side damage, the worst was yet to come.

Jerry Nadeau, who was subbing for the injured Ernie Irvan in the MB2 Motorsports Pontiac, tagged the back of Jarrett's Ford on the frontstretch, bringing out another yellow flag and sending the Robert Yates Racing Ford into the pits for lengthy repairs that would take 155 laps.

Jarrett, who began the night with a seemingly unassailable 300-point lead over Mark Martin in the Winston Cup championship, saw his margin dwindle to a still-comfortable 213 points by the end of the race.

To his credit, Jarrett took responsibility for the first wreck.

"I created the problem for some other people and myself," Jarrett said. "It was my fault."

NASCAR, however, penalized Nadeau two laps for rough driving, which did not go over well with his team and crew chief Ryan Pemberton.

"Where's the justice at?" Pemberton asked after the race. "What the 3 car did, that was blatant. I don't know, that was at least two laps, I think."

As the night wore on, rookie Stewart set the pace, leading a race-high 225 laps. But before long, the usual Bristol hijinxs started to play out.

David Green hit the turn-three wall midway through the race to bring out the yellow flag again. When the leaders all pitted on lap 252, it was Gordon out first, then Martin, Stewart, Marlin and Bobby Labonte.

Ten laps later, Kyle Petty tapped Stricklin coming out of turn four, an accident that also snared Johnny Benson.

The track went green on lap 269, and five laps later Earnhardt and Rusty Wallace had contact, causing Wallace's left rear to go down. Wallace pitted for fresh rubber on lap 278, but he was two laps down and effectively out of contention for a win.

It got worse. Chad Little spun Mayfield and collected Kenny Irwin and Wally Dallenbach in turn two on lap 290.

The green flew again on lap 296, and on the restart Stewart almost lost it in turn one as he went high, allowing Martin to retake second place.

Then Irwin brought out yet another yellow flag, getting loose into Nadeau in turn four, and wrecking half a dozen other cars in the process.

With the yellow out, the complexion of the race changed.

About half of the lead-lap car pitted on lap 300, but when the green flag came back out on lap 305, the order was jumbled by the cars that stayed out: Terry Labonte ahead of Earnhardt, Spencer, Geoffrey Bodine, Rudd, Gordon, Bobby Labonte, Stewart Martin and Marlin.

Stewart's decision to pit proved to be a good one: His right rear tire was going flat.

Then the race settled down, with veterans Labonte and Earnhardt in command out front, which is how it stayed for the final 200 laps, as they swapped the lead seven more times.

Dave Marcis slowed high on the track on lap 411, after he couldn't get an opening down low to pit. The track went yellow and NASCAR assessed Marcis a one-lap penalty for intentionally bringing out a caution.

The leaders all pitted on lap 412, with Labonte emerging ahead of teammate Gordon, Earnhardt, Stewart, Bobby Labonte, Martin, Rudd, Spencer, Little and Brett Bodine.

Labonte remained in the lead until lap 435, when Earnhardt passed him and stayed in front for four laps, before Labonte went back into the lead, a position he would hold onto until the 490th of 500 laps.

The final 10 laps were pure bedlam. Mayfield and Wally Dallenbach collided on the backstretch on lap 490, as the leaders rushed by. Labonte made it safely into turn three when he was spun by Darrell Waltrip.

"I don't know what he was thinking," a peeved Labonte said afterward.

Labonte ducked into the pits for fresh tires and seemed out of it. But with few cars left on the lead lap, he emerged from the pits fifth behind Earnhardt, Stewart, Gordon – none of whom had pitted – and Martin.

When the green flag came out again on lap 496, Labonte took off like a shot on his fresh tires, quickly passing the three cars ahead of him, Martin first, then on lap 498 getting by Gordon and Stewart, respectively.

On lap 499 he muscled past Earnhardt, bumping him a little in turns three and four. It appeared certain he was headed for victory lane. At least until Earnhardt nailed him on the last lap, that is.

"I don't think I spun Terry intentionally," Earnhardt said. "You'll have to go to NASCAR about all that. I've got big shoulders and I can take the pressure or the blame or whatever. It was not an intentional bump, but it happened.

"I'm sure we'll hear about the race for awhile, and we'll just have to take it like it is. Like I said, I have broad shoulders. I have to take what comes and race from here on.

"If it would have been on the other foot and I'd been the one turned around, I would think about it pretty hard and know he was going to race me hard to win."

John Hendrick argued driver Labonte's case afterward in the NASCAR trailer, but to no avail.

"They made their ruling, they're not going to change anything," said Hendrick. "It stands. We're not happy with it at all. Everybody saw what happened. It's a shame for Terry 'cause he fought back so hard."

Runner-up Spencer, however, may have had the definitive word on the last-lap melee.

"I went into the final turn, and wow, Ironman and Ironhead got together," he said.

And that was that. ∎

Earnhardt still savors these moments, even though there have been 73 others.

Basic Black Still In Fashion

Earnhardt Again Proves He's Master Of The Wind In Talladega Shootout

At age 48, Dale Earnhardt squelched any talk about retirement by winning the Winston 500 at Talladega in thrilling fashion, passing Dale Jarrett for the lead with just three laps remaining. It was his third win of the season, the 74th of his career, and gave him a sweep of the Talladega races for that season. "I'm not thinking about retirement by any means," Earnhardt said. "I'm still winning races and finishing in the top 10."

Dale Earnhardt set the record straight at Talladega: His fans are going to have to wait for his retirement tour. And the wait could be a lengthy one.

The seven-time Winston Cup champion is close to finalizing a new contract with car owner Richard Childress, and of course is actively involved with son Dale Jr.'s upcoming Winston Cup rookie season in 2000.

More significantly, perhaps, Earnhardt is seriously stoked about his prospects for the future, despite being 48 years old and being written off after winning just one Winston Cup race between March 1996 and the end of last season.

Reports of Earnhardt's demise, though, have proven greatly exaggerated.

This year "The Intimidator" has flashed his championship form of yesteryear, winning a bump-and-grind bash at Bristol and on this Indian Summer Alabama afternoon, he completed a Talladega sweep with a stunning victory in the Winston 500.

The Talladega victory was the 74th of Earnhardt's storied Winston Cup career, including 45 on superspeedways. In addition to sweeping both races at Talladega this year, he finished second in both Daytona races, the Daytona 500 and Pepsi 400, the only other track on which Winston Cup cars use restrictor plates.

And if you listen to Earnhardt, there's a whole lot of winning still left to be done before he even thinks about hanging up his helmet.

In the post-race interview at Talladega, he flashed as much form as he did on the track, mixing the trademark bravado with a few semi-sarcastic one-liners.

In other words, it was vintage Earnhardt.

"I'm not thinking about retirement by any means," said Earnhardt in the press box. "It's real funny to me that all of a sudden I became Dale Sr. I mean, Darrell Waltrip's the guy who's talking about retirement, not Dale Earnhardt. And I'm still winning races and running in the top 10 in points all the time and have for the last several years.

"And I don't see where I should be getting older just because Darrell is or anybody else, or I've got a son in racing now and he's Dale Jr. I shouldn't be Dale Sr. I should just be Dale Earnhardt."

Bold words, perhaps, but if Earnhardt's proven anything over his career, it's that he doesn't just talk the talk, he walks the walk, too.

"We're going to win that eighth championship, that's our No. 1 goal right now," said car owner Childress. "Dale Earnhardt can still do it, and anyone that's ever doubted it made a big mistake."

It sure seemed that way in Talladega.

A blown engine in first-day qualifying meant Earnhardt started the Winston 500 way back in 27th place. But he wasted absolutely no time going to the front.

Astonishingly, he moved all the way up to third place by lap eight and remained in contention the rest of the day.

It has been said of Earnhardt that he can see the air in the draft, and the way he drove early in this affair did little to dispel the myth.

"We started off at a deficit there at 27th, but we were rolling along there and it got sort of two-wide and then sort of opened up in the middle. I was sort of seeing some things that I thought would work. I went for it and went through the middle."

And so he did, blowing by the competition as if his black Chevrolet was the only car out there without one of those damnable restrictor plates choking back the horsepower of his engine.

But it would take awhile for Earnhardt to get all the way to the front – lap 106 of 188, to be exact – while all around chaos reigned.

From the get-go, drivers ran three-, four- and even five-wide around the giant 2.66-mile Talladega track, trading positions with wild abandon.

It looked like a 15-lap feature at some half-mile dirt track, or maybe a 200 mph rugby scrum. That the high-speed anarchy resulted in only one crash, a five-car affair midway, rather than the 20- or 30-car pileup that's come to be the norm at restrictor-plate tracks was nothing short of miraculous.

In the first 20 laps alone, eight different drivers led, as drivers repeatedly got shuffled in and out of the draft, as is the custom at Talladega.

One lap, a guy would be in the lead, the next lap he'd be hung out to dry and end up eighth or 10th or even 20th.

It happened to Earnhardt. It also happened to Dale Jarrett, Bobby Labonte, Jeff Gordon and Tony Stewart, Joe Nemechek and Sterling Marlin, all of whom at one time or another seemed to have cars capable of winning.

Gordon, in particular, looked stout, as if he could win for the third time in a row with new crew chief Brian Whitesell. He led four times for 71 laps, by far the most of any driver.

Jarrett, too, looked strong, running the car that had won this race a year earlier and the Pepsi 400 at Daytona in July.

But the only one who seemed capable of muscling his way back up front, especially late in the race, was Earnhardt.

Of course, so much depended on teamwork and temporary alliances. If drivers worked together, they could move up. Drift out of line and you went straight back.

"It's tough to pick your partner at any point of that race," Earnhardt said. "I would see guys that would be sitting in line racing and guys would pull out on you and run along on the bottom and you'd draft by 'em.

"Guys would line up and you'd get back by 'em, and you'd look in your mirror and they'd be back about 15th place. It was just a tough day. I did that one time and

Used to "cleaning up" at Talladega, Earnhardt sweeps up the funny money in victory lane.

> **"And I don't see where I should be getting older just because Darrell is or anybody else, or I've got a son in racing now and he's Dale Jr. I shouldn't be Dale Sr. I should just be Dale Earnhardt."**

slipped back to about 12th. You just had to be careful on what moves you made and when you made 'em and who was around when you made 'em."

And what set the stage for Earnhardt's final moves occurred when most of the leaders pitted for their final stops of the race. At the same time Terry Labonte suffered a punctured oil cooler in the trioval, bringing out a caution on lap 140.

Of the cars that were coming down pit road when Labonte's oil cooler blew, only Bobby Labonte, Earnhardt and Ward Burton completed their service.

The rest of the leaders pitted again on lap 142, and when the track went green on lap 146, the order was Bobby Labonte, Burton, Earnhardt, Bobby Hamilton, Michael Waltrip, Jarrett, Steve Park, Kenny Irwin, Elliott Sadler and Gordon.

Earnhardt reassumed the lead on lap 147, only to be passed by the surprising Waltrip after just three laps. Unfortunately for Waltrip, his stay up front was short, as he blew an engine on lap 155, one lap after Jarrett passed him to take the lead.

During the last 35 laps, Jarrett led twice for 20 laps and appeared ready to back up last year's victory here.

By his own admission, Earnhardt didn't have the best car, but he again proved he is the master of the draft.

"As far as seeing air, I know it's there," he said. "I've just got to play the hunches right and hope it's there when I need it."

And that he did.

As the laps wound down, RCR teammate Mike Skinner and Labonte hooked up with Earnhardt to get up front. And on lap 185, the black No. 3 made the decisive pass of Jarrett for the win.

"Jarrett was hanging tough on the bottom. I knew it was going to be tough to get by him," Earnhardt said. "Skinner and the 18 car (Labonte) worked hard and helped me get up there. Once I cleared the 88 (Jarrett), I tried to pull Skinner with me and he got hung up with the 88. The 18 got to racing and got by him.

"Then, they got to going three-wide. It was getting down to the last two laps and everybody was panicking. They were making all the moves they could."

But as he so often does, Earnhardt had the last word about holding off the competition from up front.

"You can play defense better than you can play offense from the back," he said.

As the checkered flag fell, Earnhardt scored his third win this season and ninth of his career at Talladega, giving him a sweep of both 1999 Winston Cup races at the Alabama superspeedway.

Earnhardt set a blistering pace all afternoon, averaging 166.632 mph in the 188-lap race, which saw a whopping 32 lead changes among 16 drivers, and only three cautions for 17 laps.

Finishing second just 0.114 second behind Earnhardt was Jarrett, who took a giant step toward clinching his first Winston Cup championship, leaving with a 246-point lead over Bobby Labonte.

Ricky Rudd came home third, followed by Ward Burton, Kenny Wallace, Stewart and Labonte. Rounding out the top 10 were Jeff Burton in the Roush Racing Ford, the Morgan McClure Motorsports Chevrolet of Hamilton and Kenny Irwin in the Robert Yates Racing Ford. ■

Earnhardt Rules

Veteran Beats Labonte By Inches In A Classic Finish

Earnhardt's 75th career Cup victory was no doubt one of his most exciting, as he beat Bobby Labonte by mere inches to earn his ninth Atlanta win. The battle capped a 13-lap run to the finish with both cars crossing the line side by side and sending officials scurrying to the video replay to determine the winner.

For a few seconds after the checkered flag fell on the Cracker Barrel Old Country Store 500, no one was quite sure who had won.

Dale Earnhardt's Richard Childress Racing crew stood along pit road with bewildered looks on their faces.

Bobby Labonte's Joe Gibbs Racing team wasn't too sure, either.

There was no roar from the fans, and the media in the press box looked at each other and asked, "Who won?"

Finally, the RCR crewmen released shouts of joy. Earnhardt had been declared the winner in what can be defined as a classic stock car race; the kind of race that rocketed NASCAR Winston Cup racing to national popularity.

And the type of race NASCAR needed after the reaction it had received from many fans and media members who had called the first three events of the season boring.

For the cool, sunny day, Hollywood couldn't have written a better script as the maturing youngster

battled the seasoned veteran for the victory. Side by side they raced off turn four for the checkered flag with the fans cheering wildly. For NASCAR's camera located at the finish line, it became a victory frozen in time.

Labonte had no idea who had won. "I couldn't tell," he said in his post-race interview.

Earnhardt, however, felt he was the winner.

"When we were getting close to the line, I looked over and his car wasn't really side by side with me as far as looking into the driver's door … so I felt pretty good about what our chances were that we beat him out by a nose," Earnhardt said.

He was correct. He had collected his 75th career win by inches, and some might argue by the two inches NASCAR allowed the Chevrolet teams to extend their front air dam.

"I just came up about a valence too short, two inches too short, whatever you want to call it," a disappointed Labonte said. "It's just one of those deals. I haven't seen the replay and don't really care to. It doesn't really matter to me. I just ended up a little short."

Since the fall of 1996, the track had belonged to the 35-year-old Labonte, who had celebrated victory in four of the last seven races. The 48-year-old Earnhardt, meanwhile, hadn't won at the speedway since the spring of '96 and not since it had been reconfigured into a 1.54-mile track for the 1997 season.

In this 325-lap event, Earnhardt was better on the short runs and Labonte held the advantage on the long ones.

With 13 laps remaining, the race restarted from its final caution flag, and it was clear it would be a two-car battle.

On lap 316, Labonte challenged Earnhardt on the outside on the backstretch, and they raced side by side through turns three and four. Earnhardt pulled back ahead as they began lap 317.

Labonte elected to follow Earnhardt until he saw the white flag. It was now or never, and this time Labonte elected to try the low groove, inching ahead of Earnhardt, who went high in turns three and four. They never touched as each driver held his line through the dogleg and to the checkered flag.

"I was just running the outside in (turns) one and two better than I was running the outside in (turns) three and four," Labonte said. "I could get up off of two better than I could get up off of four. So I was running through one and two high.

"On the last lap, Dale moved up a little bit. I still had a good run off the corner. It really bit on the rear, and I had a run on him. I got right on his back bumper down the back straightaway. I knew he was going to go high because I had been running up there, and it was just kind of how the trend had been going all day. I had no option but to go low.

"You really don't stick that good down low. But I guess I had run high long enough that my tires

stuck a little bit better than I anticipated. I didn't even figure I'd get close to his rear bumper to be honest with you. When it stuck, I got back on the gas as hard as I could and just used up all the race track I could to get down to the start/finish line as fast as I could."

Earnhardt, who noted he and Labonte almost wrecked when Skinner's engine blew and left oil in turns one and two, described the last lap as "good racin'."

"I got after it as hard as I could there at the end and ran hard," he said. "I found a pretty good line through (turns) three and four. In (turns) one and two, I was on the bottom. In three and four, I was up a little bit. I held him off.

"It sort of seemed he was waiting, biding his time. Sure enough, he made his run there on the last lap and got close to beating us. It definitely wasn't a boring race."

It wasn't until the race's second half that Labonte and Earnhardt became factors in the event. Skinner, Earnhardt's teammate, had dominated and appeared headed for his first-ever Winston Cup win before his car's engine blew with 20 laps remaining. He led eight times for 191 laps and at one point drew the ire of his teammate.

On lap 207, Earnhardt moved to the inside of Skinner as they headed for turn three. Skinner cut him off, clipping Earnhardt's left front. Earnhardt later said it was too early to be using those tactics; Skinner felt he was justified with the maneuver.

"I'd wreck my mom to win my first race," Skinner said. "Dale did what he had to do, and I did what I had to do. He's my teammate and I wouldn't wreck him, and it was too early in the race to be wrecking anybody, but I blocked him. He probably was further alongside me than I thought."

Earnhardt said he was angry with Skinner for bending his right front fender.

Earnhardt held Bobby Labonte at bay by mere inches at the finish.

Earnhardt celebrates his 75th career victory with retired Gen. Colin Powell. Earnhardt lists Powell as one of his heroes.

"It was too early to be racing like that," he said. "I was under him coming off the corner, and as I was coming off the corner, he kept coming down and kept coming down, and I just kept going and going. We finally got together, and I was past the stripe on the inside. It just didn't need to happen at that stage of the race. We had two good race cars, and we could have torn them up right there."

While Skinner and Earnhardt fans will argue over who was right and who was wrong, it was the finish that probably will cause intense arguments to erupt among Ford and General Motors fans. Even Earnhardt admitted he couldn't have won with the Monte Carlo he raced the previous week.

"I think it would have pushed too much through the center and off the corner," he said. "I think we've got a better race car (now) to race with, and our balance is better than what we had. We just need to keep tuning on it."

One thing that possibly helped Earnhardt in the race was crew chief Kevin Hamlin's planning ahead. Hamlin was aware activities at the track might get rained out the day before the event. He called Earnhardt and asked if he had any problem with them practicing some race runs on pole day rather than just concentrating on qualifying. Earnhardt had no objections.

"Our plan was to get a little bit of race practice in and have an idea of what this new valence change was going to do for us, especially here at Atlanta," Hamlin said. "I think it was a good thing for our whole team to do that, and it paid off for us today."

Still, when they began the race they were quite loose.

"We put a rubber in on the right front on the first pit stop that we had taken out and adjusted it a little bit with wedge and track bar," Earnhardt said. "We adjusted a little bit, as we went, really not a lot after that.

"We were really afraid to do too much one way or the other because we were worried about one set of tires being too tight or loose. We just sort of stayed there and it worked out for us. We had a consistent race car once we got all the fenders knocked back out straight and quit running over things."

Earnhardt also noted speedway officials "messed up a good race track when they put this dogleg in it."

"But that's their choice. They bought the race track, they can do what they want to with it," he said. "It's a good race track, but it was a great race track before. It's an OK race track now. It's a lot different than it was. That dogleg is not a favorite of mine, neither here nor Texas nor Charlotte."

For the owner of seven Winston Cup championships, the win was special. Not just because it was his ninth one at Atlanta, but because retired Gen. Colin Powell was in attendance.

"I've always been a big fan of his and how he worked hard for the American way and for the dream that we have," Earnhardt said. "To get to meet him today at the drivers meeting and then to get to receive the trophy from him was a great honor. That's going to be something that will go down in my scrapbook. Maybe I can get him to autograph a picture for me. That was neat because he was here today." ■

"I haven't seen the replay and don't really care to. It doesn't really matter to me. I just ended up a little short." —Bobby Labonte

Crowd Pleaser

Earnhardt Puts On A Show In Yet Another Talladega Triumph

His last victory was one of the most impressive. Sure, Earnhardt was a master of restrictor-plate racing, but even this was incredible. While the draft was in play at Talladega at the time, it was not as easy to move to the front as it is today. Sitting in 16th with six laps remaining, Earnhardt weaved his way to the win. Kenny Wallace played a key role in pushing him to the win. Victory No. 76 came five races before Earnhardt's death in the 2001 Daytona 500.

Dale Earnhardt hates restrictor-plate racing. Always has. Always will. And that's not going to change no matter how many times he wins at NASCAR's biggest track.

The day before the Winston 500, he said they'd taken racing out of the drivers' hands here years ago when they first bolted carburetor plates on the cars. So the fact that NASCAR changed the size of the plate less than 24 hours before the race was something he could shrug off as just another reason to hate plate racing.

Yet the more he gripes about it, the more determined he seems to go out and prove himself wrong. In another trademark performance, Earnhardt maneuvered from 22nd to the lead in the final, frantic 10 laps on the way to his 10th career win at Talladega Superspeedway. If that's not the mark of a great driver, nothing is.

Earnhardt may not truly see the air as has long been discussed, but he sure can see the way to the front when it matters most.

Just don't ask how he got there. Or what he thinks of restrictor plates. Not even winning Winston's No Bull 5 $1 million bonus could change his opinion.

"I still don't like restrictor-plate racing," he said. "I'm not that good at it."

Well, if he ever gets to the level he considers proficient, the other 42 drivers ought to take the afternoon off. But if that happened, fans wouldn't know what to do at Daytona and Talladega. If Earnhardt's not leading, the most fun is watching his black Chevrolet to see how he gets to the front.

You pretty much have to watch for yourself. And you should probably take notes – or have the VCR running at home – because even Earnhardt had a hard time explaining exactly how he won for the 76th time in a legendary career. It was simply that spectacular.

One minute he was nowhere to be seen, up to just 16th with six laps left, then he was blowing by Richard Childress Racing teammate Mike Skinner with two laps remaining for the lead. He then outran drafting partners Kenny Wallace and Joe Nemechek to the stripe, while Skinner was shuffled to sixth behind Jeff Gordon and Terry Labonte.

"I don't know how I won it, honestly," Earnhardt said. "We had moved up and got pushed back again. I was up and down there between 10 and 15 (laps) to go. To be 18th or wherever we were with five to go is pretty impressive and says a lot for the rules and spotters and everything to make the racing more competitive. The problem is, it's hard to move

The Talladega straightaway looks like rush hour on the freeway as Dale Earnhardt and his son, Dale Jr., lead the pack.

through these cars. You've got to work your way around and by them.

"We just were fortunate to get hooked up with Kenny and Joe Nemechek there and work our way to the front. Basically, that's how I won the race, because Kenny and Joe got in there and all three Chevrolets got together and worked their way to the front."

Childress, Earnhardt and Andy Petree, who owns the cars of Wallace and Nemechek, have an engineering alliance to help the cars aerodynamically. But thoughts of being teammates in some broad sense played no role in the outcome. Wallace simply knew the best chance for his first Winston Cup win would come by working with Earnhardt on the way to the front.

Success is a drink best served cold; and in an oversized champagne bottle.

> ## "I hit Earnhardt once square and I knocked the hell out of him three or four times and I personally won the race for him." —Kenny Wallace

That's why he kept bump-drafting with the seven-time champion.

"I had no choice but to hit him and keep pushing him into the lead," Wallace said.

"... I was doing everything but hitting him through the trioval. I realized once I hit him I wasn't going to lift him. Sometimes you hit these guys and it lifts them up. I hit Earnhardt once square and I knocked the hell out of him three or four times and I personally won the race for him."

Earnhardt had help beyond that provided by Wallace and Nemechek, including some from his son. On a day when NASCAR's new aerodynamic rules helped produce 49 lead changes among 21 drivers, it appeared Earnhardt Jr. might post his third career win until John Andretti got by on lap 185. Skinner led the next circuit before things got even crazier than normal.

Earnhardt Jr. tried getting a run on Skinner and got down on the apron alongside him before thinking better of the maneuver, which might have triggered a huge wreck had he forced the issue. Still, Skinner had to check up for an instant, which is when Earnhardt got back in front.

"Dad just got a great run on the outside," Earnhardt Jr. said. "Skinner was not going to win the race in the position he was in, so I either had to get by him or finish behind him."

Master that he is, Wallace and Nemechek simply couldn't make a move on Earnhardt, whose win was greeted with a rousing ovation from the faithful, many of whom rarely sat the entire day.

And while many were fans of the racing brought on by the new aero package, not all were smiling.

"It's 43 cars that look like they're in a parking lot," groused Frankie Stoddard, Jeff Burton's crew chief. "You could take a picture of the road that goes to Oxford, Ala. that's four lanes wide, and that would look exactly what it was like watching this race. Boring. Boring. Boring."

Considering Chevrolets swept the top six spots and Burton's Ford finished 29th after losing a lap to a cut tire, Stoddard's sentiments are understandable. But it wasn't just the Ford contingent griping.

Jimmy Makar, crew chief for points leader Labonte, was rather displeased after his driver got shuffled back to 12th during the furious finish.

"It was exactly what we expected," Makar said. "(NASCAR) got what they wanted, a bunch of junk. We'd accomplish the same thing in a 10-lap or a 25-lap race here. It's all the same. It ain't about good race cars, it's about a chess match: who makes the right move, who makes the wrong move; who slips, who doesn't. That's what happened there at the end. Little E got down on the bottom, slipped, about wrecked, caused one line to slow up and the other line went, and that's all it took.

"It's not about racing to me here. It never has been since they've gone to this kind of restrictor plate racing. It's great for the fans, I know. It's a great show. But it's not much fun racing."

It was certainly harrowing at times, not to mention nostalgic. Dave Marcis led the second lap after starting ninth, Bill Elliott ran like it was 1988 and Ken Schrader had moments where it looked like he might earn his